INTRODUCING
CHRISTIAN
ETHICS

OTHER BOOKS BY SCOTT B. RAE

The Ethics of Commercial Surrogate Motherhood:
Brave New Families? (Praeger Publishing, 1994)

Moral Choices: An Introduction to Ethics (Zondervan, 1995;
2nd Edition, 2000; 3rd Edition, 2009)

Brave New Families: Biblical Ethics and Reproductive Technologies
(Baker Book House, 1996)

Beyond Integrity: A Judeo-Christian Approach to
Business Ethics, with Kenman L. Wong. (Zondervan,
1996; 2nd Edition, 2004; 3rd Edition, 2012)

Embryo Research and Experimentation
(Crossroads Monograph Series on Faith and Policy, 1997)

Bioethics: A Christian Approach in a Pluralistic Culture,
with Paul M. Cox (Eerdmans/Paternoster, 1999)

Body and Soul: Human Nature and the Crisis in Ethics,
with J. P. Moreland (InterVarsity Press, 2000)

Biotechnology and the Human Good,
with C. Ben Mitchell et al. (Georgetown University Press, 2007)

The Virtues of Capitalism: A Moral Case for Free Markets,
with Austin Hill (Northfield Publications, 2011)

Business for the Common Good,
with Kenman L. Wong (IVP Academic, 2011)

Outside the Womb: Moral Guidance for Assisted Reproduction,
with D. Joy Riley, MD (Moody Press, 2012)

Doing the Right Thing: Making Moral Choices
in a World Full of Options (Zondervan, 2013)

INTRODUCING CHRISTIAN ETHICS

A Short Guide to Making Moral Choices

Scott B.
RAE

ZONDERVAN

Introducing Christian Ethics
Copyright © 2016 by Scott B. Rae

An abridgment of *Moral Choices*

This title is also available as a Zondervan ebook.

Requests for information should be addressed to:
Zondervan, 3900 *Sparks Drive SE, Grand Rapids, Michigan 49546*

Library of Congress Cataloging-in-Publication Data

Names: Rae, Scott B., author. | Rae, Scott B., author. Moral choices.
Title: Introducing Christian ethics : a short guide to making moral choices / Scott B.
    Rae.
Description: Grand Rapids : Zondervan, 2016. | Abridgement of: Moral choices.
Identifiers: LCCN 2016017309 | ISBN 9780310521181 (softcover)
Subjects: LCSH: Christian ethics
Classification: LCC BJ1251 .R236 2016 | DDC 241--dc23 LC record available at
    https://lccn.loc.gov/2016017309

Any italics in Scripture quotations are added by the author for emphasis.

Cover Image: Superstock.com
Interior design: Kait Lamphere

Printed in the United States of America

HB 04.30.2024

CONTENTS

CHAPTER 1

STARTING AT THE BEGINNING

What's so good about being good?

Imagine that you live in a world where you can do anything you want, and no matter what you do, you will never get caught. Nor will you ever have to worry about any consequences for these actions. For example, you can rob a bank, cheat in school, take revenge on whomever you want to, commit violent crimes, lie whenever you want, go back on your word whenever convenient, or sleep with whomever you choose. Would you do any, or all, of those things? I suspect many of you would be tempted to do at least some things commonly regarded as immoral, not to mention some of the illegal things. But I also suspect most of you would not do them. Why not? Although you might not be able to express it precisely, I would bet that many people would not do these things because they consider being a good person to be an important part of living a good life. That is, you consider it a good thing to be a good person.

MORALITY AND THE GOOD LIFE

But let's think about that a bit more. What is it about morality, or virtue, that is bound up with living a good life? The ancient philosophers affirmed that being a good person and living a good life went together and that success in life was measured by what kind of person you were as opposed to what you accomplished or accumulated. For example, Aristotle connected happiness with being a good person. He said, "Happiness is an activity of the soul *in accordance with virtue.*" Epicurus put it this way: "It is not possible to live pleasantly without living *prudently, honorably and justly.*" This certainly reflects the teaching of Jesus himself when he said to his disciples, "What good is it for someone to gain the whole world, yet forfeit their soul [a part of which includes their character]?" (Mark 8:36).

Even today, most people, at least intuitively, make that connection between good character and a good life. This is why we admire the moral heroes of our time, and conversely, why we look skeptically at someone who achieves much but is devoid of character. For example, Mother Teresa remains one of the most admired people in the world, even though she had little of what counts for success in our culture. On the other hand, the person who is at the top of his or her profession but who got there by running over people, has had multiple failed marriages, and is alienated from his or her children—we have a harder time thinking of this person as being successful in life. We often say of this person that "they got to the top of the ladder, only to realize it was leaning against the wrong wall."

I heard a vivid example of this when I was a PhD student some years ago. It made an indelible impact on me, and I vowed not to repeat the mistakes I had learned about. I was the teaching assistant for a distinguished professor in our department, and part of that responsibility involved attending all the class sessions. On the final day of class for that term, the professor was making a point and used his personal life as an example. He told his students about how he had ordered his life early in his career, when his children were young. He spoke with great regret about how he had spent far too many evenings and weekends in his study, writing books and articles to establish himself professionally, at which he had succeeded, since he was well respected in his field. But he also spoke of how he was alienated from all his children today, and it broke his heart to recognize that those two things were connected. I suspect he would admit that he was a professional success but that no amount of professional success compensated for his failures as a father. He realized that professional success and life success were two different things. I suspect he might have seen himself in Jesus's statement, "What good is it for someone to gain the whole world, yet forfeit their soul?"

WE ARE MORAL BEINGS

So we tend to connect being moral to having a good life. That's a good reason to be moral. But that's not the only reason to think morality is important. From a Christian worldview, *morality is built into the fabric of the universe and is built into our constitution as human beings.* It is an integral part of what it means to be human. This is certainly the idea of the moral law being written on our hearts, as described in Romans 2:14–15. Paul here is arguing for the pervasiveness and universality of sin by maintaining that we all violate God's law, whether we have access to it or not: "Indeed, when Gentiles, who do not have the law, do by nature things required by the law, they are a law for themselves, even though they do not have the law. They show that the requirements of the law *are written on their hearts*, their consciences also bearing witness, and their thoughts sometimes accusing them and at other times even defending them."

The point of the text is that the demands of morality are imprinted internally on each person, giving him or her an inherent sense of right and wrong. This is one way that God communicates the requirement of morality. As we will see in chapter 2, in the discussion of natural law ethics, God reveals his moral program for human beings in a variety of ways, both inside and outside the Bible. Of course, this does not mean that everyone always sees morality the same way, since, in a Christian worldview, our moral constitution is also broken because of the reality of sin in the world. (We will discuss other ways of viewing morality, including relativism, in chapter 3.) But sin did not eradicate the moral sense of human beings; that moral sense remains part and parcel of what it means to be human. In this sense, asking the question, why be moral? is a bit like asking, why be human? It's not something we can avoid. We can't not be moral beings, since it's who we are.

This is why it makes sense to connect being moral with being a good person and having a good life, and ultimately with being a human being. In the same way that we are rational, conscious, and relational, created by a rational, conscious, and relational God, we are also moral beings created by a moral God. It is part of who we are, because we are created by a particular kind of God who embedded morality in the fabric of the universe, including the fabric of each person's makeup.

I admit that this is not what people usually are asking when they inquire, "Why be moral?" What they are asking is, "Why should I do what I know to be right?" Or to put it differently, "Why should I be a good person?" What makes this a difficult question is that doing the right thing usually involves some sort of sacrifice of a person's self-interest. If it didn't, we wouldn't be having this discussion! If doing the right thing were always in our perceived self-interest, we would always do the right thing, and there would be no such things as temptations or ethical dilemmas. You certainly wouldn't be reading a book about ethics, because you would easily do what's right, since it would always benefit you. But at least in the short term, that's not necessarily or even normally true. Most ethical decisions come with some cost, though in the long term, a better case can be made for the benefit of being ethical, as we will maintain in the later chapter about business ethics.

MORALITY AND THE GOOD SOCIETY

We've already connected being moral with being a good person and living a good life, which makes sense, since a moral awareness is built into each of us, and morality is part of being human. What other reasons are there to make us think that being moral is important?

Let's look at the bigger picture, beyond our individual lives, and see society as a whole. Think about what it would be like to live in a culture where no one cared about morality. In fact, morality is so deeply embedded in our humanity that it is difficult even to envision a society in which morality is ignored. Even those parts of the world that exist outside the control of government and the law still have moral requirements that bind their communities together, and often they are very strong. A culture devoid of morality reminds me of Gotham City in the Batman films, or the William Golding novel which you may have read in school, *Lord of the Flies*. In that novel, preadolescent kids create their own society on an island, and it quickly degenerates into a "might makes right" culture and becomes a horror story in which only the strong survive.

The intuition of most readers of that novel is that this is a very undesirable kind of society in which no one would choose to live. Even if we may have trouble considering what a society without morality would look like, *most people have no trouble seeing that they wouldn't want to live in a culture in which morality was not taken seriously.* We may disagree about the details of morality, but we are clear on the connection between morality and a good society. In fact, our moral debates show that we care deeply about morality and consider it an important part of our community life. Take our discussions of injustice, as an example. Our most passionate cultural discussions are about injustices, either real or perceived, demonstrating how much we care about morality at the societal level. Imagine being concerned about injustice, or being a victim of injustice, in a society that didn't take morality seriously.

Even disciplines such as politics and economics are fundamentally moral enterprises. Politics is, at its core, about how we order our lives together in community. Economics is, at its core, about how we distribute the burdens and benefits of our lives together in community. Both are intrinsically moral projects because they are discussions about how we *ought* to live our lives together. From a Christian worldview, we would expect this, as a result of morality being built into the structure of the world God has made.

MORALITY AND FOLLOWING JESUS

For most believers, and consistent with a Christian worldview, *morality matters because God highly recommends being a moral person.* The Bible is clear that following Jesus involves a commitment to Christian morality. This is why some branches of Christianity call ethics "moral theology." The numerous New Testament (NT) passages that have the phrase "one another" in them are prescriptions about how to treat one another, summarized in the mandate to "love your neighbor as yourself" (Gal. 5:14; see also Col. 3:13 and Eph. 4:32). The Bible calls believers to adopt a lifestyle that reflects who they are in Christ (Eph. 4:20–5:20; Col. 3:1–17) and to imitate Christ in his character. In fact, the consummate expression of the character of Jesus that people who belong to Christ are called to develop is the "fruit of the Spirit" (Gal. 5:22–25). Thus following Jesus and cultivating the virtues of his character go closely together, suggesting that the moral life and life with Jesus are inseparable.

The Old Testament (OT) statement of the demand for individuals and communities to be moral comes in two primary ways—the commands to obey God's law (Ex. 19:5–6) and the mandate to follow the way of wisdom (Prov. 8:1, 22–31). The prophets had a good deal to say about the morality of the community, and this reinforced the law by calling Israel to account for its failure to follow the law fully. The Wisdom Literature, especially the book of Proverbs, frames the moral life in terms of the life of wisdom and calls all human beings, regardless of their worldview, to a life of wisdom. As opposed to the Mosaic law, which was intended for the nation of Israel, the wisdom books were written for more of an international audience. This helps explain why many of the distinctly Israelite theological themes, such as the ceremonial law, the Promised Land, and the covenant with Abraham, are absent from the Wisdom Literature. We can see the proverbs as an application of the law to a cross-cultural context, calling people around the world to the moral life as a commitment to the way of wisdom.

MAKING MORAL ASSESSMENTS

You may be wondering why the term morality is being used here instead of the common term *ethics*. Most people don't see much difference between the two and often use the words interchangeably. Technically, they describe two slightly different aspects of our subject. I am using the terms this way: *morality* refers to the content of right and wrong, while *ethics* refers to the discipline of discovering morality. Ethics is more the "how we get there," and morality is the "what the standards are." In other words, morality has to do with where the bar is set, and ethics is the process of figuring out where to set the bar. I use the term *discovering morality* intentionally, since morality is not fundamentally a human creation. Rather it has a transcendent source, in a Christian worldview, in the character and commands of God. That means morality is something discerned, not created. This goes strongly against the cultural consensus today which insists that we are able to make up our own moral rules for ourselves. We will explore this notion more fully in chapter 3.

I am assuming that we all make moral assessments regularly, and that is a good thing. Culturally, we are often told that we shouldn't make moral judgments about persons and things other than ourselves, that it is narrow and judgmental to do so. Some people even invoke Jesus's statement, "Do not judge, or you too will be judged" (Matt. 7:1). To be clear, Jesus is not suggesting that no one make moral assessments. Rather he maintains that we not do it hypocritically. That is, if you read the rest of the passage (vv. 3–5), you will see that Jesus teaches that we are to remove the speck from our brother's eye (a figure of speech for moral assessment and correction) but that we not ignore the log in our own eye, suggesting that we not try to assess and correct other people's bad behavior while at the same time being ignorant of our own shortcomings.

In my observation of our culture, I find that some of the most ardent advocates of not judging are themselves some of the most judgmental and intolerant toward people who disagree with them on their most deeply felt moral issues. Of course, Jesus also calls his followers to make moral assessments carefully, not judgmentally or in a condescending way, and with compassion and sensitivity.

The idea that we shouldn't make moral judgments, or assessments (the term I prefer), sounds appealing on the surface, but if you think about it, it doesn't quite hold up. In reality, we make moral assessments routinely in our lives. We make character assessments regularly, for example, when we choose to trust someone, do business with someone, hire someone, or write letters of recommendation for someone. The reason why we don't often see it as such is that we hold many of our moral assessments in common with our neighbors. Though we do see many things differently in terms of morality, we also have a reservoir of shared values that enables us to live together peacefully.

Not only do we regularly make moral assessments; we think that's a good thing. Imagine what the world would be like if no one ever made moral assessments about anything. If everyone adhered to the maxim "Don't judge," we would have chaos before long. That would be to believe, in effect, that there should be no enforcement of any restraints on people doing whatever they want to do. The only way that would work is if we all lived in self-sufficient isolation on desert islands, never needing to interact with anyone else. But that is not the way life works in the real world. For example, if we didn't assess lying as wrong and didn't uphold truth telling as a virtue, it wouldn't be long before meaningful communication would cease to exist, since we couldn't expect the truth from each other. In addition, if we didn't uphold trust and trustworthiness as virtues and didn't assess fraud as morally wrong, our ability to do business together would be severely restricted. Further, if we didn't assess injustice as morally wrong or uphold the sacredness of human life or have moral judgments against theft, the fabric of a peaceable society would soon come unraveled. Or imagine parenting young children without making moral assessments.

The reality is that we can't, and wouldn't choose to, live in a culture devoid of moral assessment. That's not to say that such assessment should be done in a condescending way that lacks compassion. Nor is it to say that moral assessment is only negative—focusing on the "thou shalt not" aspects. Equally if not more important are the virtues that are upheld as morally praiseworthy and as examples to be passed on to our children.

When it comes to moral assessment, several things need to be evaluated. Obviously, the *action*, or behavior, in question needs to be considered. That's what most people think of when making a moral assessment. But that's not all that needs to be considered. The *motive* also is important, assuming that we can know someone's motive. Sometimes the motive is all that distinguishes between two otherwise identical actions. Take, for example, the difference between a gift and a bribe. They could look exactly the same but be entirely different things, one praiseworthy and the other immoral, simply based on different motives.

Of course, frequently the motive can't be determined, which makes assessing the motive a dangerous form of speculation. In addition, it is helpful to assess the *consequences* of the action, again, as far as they can be known. Considering the outcome of the action does not necessarily make someone a utilitarian in the way they view ethics (more on this in chapter 3). This is only to say here that the outcome can be evaluated from a moral point of view, and when it can, it completes the assessment.

Finally, it is important to assess the *character* of the person involved in the action you are considering. Of course, this involves caution and sensitivity, since there may be many things about the person's character that we don't know. But we make these assessments often, particularly when we say things like, "She's acting out of character." Further, we often intuitively make these character assessments when we enter relationships that involve trust and trustworthiness.

MORALITY AND THE LAW

It is quite common today for people to assume, "If it's legal, it's moral." In addition, you will regularly hear people assert, "You can't legislate morality," frequently as the basis for opposing a public policy proposal that has a religious basis, such as a law that would restrict abortion or physician-assisted suicide. Statements like these raise the contentious issue of the relationship between morality and the law.

Simply put, *the law is the moral minimum*. It is the moral floor, not the ceiling. Most questions of morality involve this question: how far above and beyond the law does morality require us to go? Many actions that the law allows are clearly immoral. Take adultery, for example. I would not suggest using the maxim "If it's legal, it's moral" as a defense for a cheating spouse. Periodically, the law actually conflicts with the demands of morality. For example, many physicians would have great difficulty with a law or regulatory standard that would force them to perform elective abortions, participate in assisted suicide, or assist in legal executions. In addition, they would have great difficulty with the law requiring them to refer those patients to someone who will provide those services. In those cases, hopefully rare, physicians are obligated to follow the demands of morality reflected in their conscience and recognize that at times they "must obey God rather than human beings" (Acts 4:19; 5:29).

The notion that you can't legislate morality is partially true. If what this means is that no one can legislate *a moral intent*, or *motive*, that is certainly true. Generally, the law can't regulate a person's thoughts and intentions, though that is not to say that some people today are not trying to have the law regulate those too. But if it means that *moral behavior* can't be legislated, that is false, because it's done all the time. As Martin Luther King Jr. ironically put it, "The law can't stop someone from hating me, but it can stop someone from killing me."

Virtually every law has a moral foundation. Even something as simple as driving on the correct side of the road presumes the moral principle of respect for life and property. We rightly assume that someone who drives on the wrong side of the freeway has respect for neither life nor property. In addition, virtually every law is legislating someone's morality. It is a common allegation that religious people are doing something inappropriate by imposing their values via the law. However, it's not only religious people who are doing this; non-religious people are routinely imposing their values via the law.

Today the most flagrant imposition of values is being done by people advancing a secular agenda. To accuse religious groups and individuals of imposing their morality on society is, at the least, not to notice that "the emperor is wearing no clothes!" and, at worst, blatant hypocrisy. Religious groups and individuals attempting to influence public policy do not violate the separation of church and state, since the "wall of separation" proposed was to keep the state out of the church, not to keep the church out of public policy. That is, the state was not to regulate religious belief, and religious freedom includes the freedom to influence culture by a variety of means, mainly moral persuasion but also including the law.

That is not to say that all sin should be illegal. Some things should be left to consenting adults to make choices on their own, apart from interference of the law. Generally, something should be a matter of law when it's necessary to avoid tangible and significant harm to others and when essential civil rights are at stake. Thus I would argue that the law is appropriate for abortion and assisted suicide, since there are essential rights to life at stake, but not for sexual matters among consenting adults.

CONCLUSION

In this chapter, we've tried to answer the question, what's so good about being good? We've suggested that being a good person is bound up with both living a good life and creating a good society.

We further argued that being a morally good person is an integral part of faithfully following Jesus. Moral assessment is something we all do routinely, whether we know it or not, and includes evaluating the action, the motive behind it, the consequences of the action, and the character of the person doing it. The law, though valuable, is only the moral minimum, and it's important to recognize that virtually all law has a moral foundation that gives it social credibility.

Review Questions

1. How would you answer the question posed at the beginning of this chapter—what's so good about being good?
2. When making moral assessments, what must be assessed in addition to the action being performed?
3. What is the connection between morality and the law?

For Further Reading

Rae, Scott B. *Doing the Right Thing: Making Moral Choices in a World Full of Options.* Grand Rapids: Zondervan, 2012.

CHAPTER 2

THEOLOGICAL ETHICS

Where does morality come from?

When we get into discussions about moral issues, especially controversial ones, it is not uncommon to hear the objection raised to the effect of, "Says who?" That is, when a claim about right or wrong is advanced, a common counterargument is to press the question of moral authority for that claim. "Who says X is wrong?" is the frequent response that often stops the conversation. In making that objection, the person is raising a very important question concerning where morality comes from.

Christian ethics has clear answers to this question that connect well with our common moral intuitions. In this chapter, we will answer the question about the origin of morality and describe ethics from a distinctly Christian worldview. We will outline the main elements of a Christian ethic and describe how the moral demands of a Christian ethic are communicated, both in God's Word and in God's world, the latter known as natural law. A Christian ethic is one that is objective, universal, and transcendent, a view known roughly as "moral realism." A Christian ethic also is portrayed not simply as a matter of opinion but as facts and knowledge.

MORALITY AND GOD'S CHARACTER

In answer to the question, "where does morality come from?" the Bible is clear that morality is *ultimately* grounded in the character of God. God's commands in the Scripture are important, but not the ultimate source of morality. Rather, they are a penultimate source for morality. That is, they are very important and close to the ultimate source, but just below the character of God. In a Christian ethic, we are called to the moral life because God is a moral God who has hardwired us for moral action. This is what we meant in chapter 1 when we said that all human beings have an innate moral sense. We are fundamentally moral beings, because we were created by a moral God who wove morality into the fabric of his world. We are called to specific character traits because God exhibits those traits, and Jesus modeled them in his earthly life.

The Bible repeatedly links God's character with our moral obligations. For example, we are to be holy, *as God is holy* (Lev. 20:26). Jesus repeats this in the NT when he maintains that we are to be perfect, *as God is perfect* (Matt. 5:48). To be more specific, God calls his people to avoid showing partiality, *because God is impartial* in his dealings with human beings (Rom. 2:11; James 2:5–8). God calls us to be forgiving people, *because he is a forgiving God* by virtue of Christ (Eph. 4:32). It is also true that the exercise of these traits produces many good outcomes—love does make the world go around! We would expect that, given how God has embedded morality in his world. But at the core, we develop moral character because God is that kind of a God.

To be sure, God's commands are a very important source of our moral obligations. We have the commands we do precisely because God is the kind of God that he is. His commands spell out the behavior that is consistent with his character. There are things that God cannot command because they are inconsistent with his character. But his commands follow from his character; they are not independent of it. We affirm this when we answer the long-standing

Euthyphro dilemma. The ancient Greeks posed a quandary to believers in the Greek gods, which has been a repeated challenge to theistic religions such as Islam, Judaism, and Christianity. It goes like this: does God command things because they are good, or are things good because God commands them?

Either answer would presumably put the believer in a difficult position. For if God commands things because they are good, that makes his commands redundant and unnecessary. But if things are good because God commands them, that puts God in the position of being able to command anything, making him potentially capricious and arbitrary.

Both "horns of the dilemma" are problematic for religious morality. However, the dilemma is eased by denying the premise—that morality is ultimately grounded in God's commands. Theologically, that's not the case, since morality is, in the end, grounded in God's *character*. We hold this when responding to the *Euthyphro*, particularly the notion that God could be capricious and arbitrary. If morality is rooted in God's character, then God cannot command anything contrary to his character. For example, the objector could say that if God's command makes things right, then if he commanded that we torture babies for fun, that would be right. But a God of the character of the biblical God would not command anything like that, since he is bound by his righteousness. In making that rejoinder, we are maintaining that the ultimate foundation for morality is God's character, not his commands. They are the *penultimate* source of right and wrong. Of course, God's character and his commands are consistent. That's why God's commands do not violate his character, and thus the reason why God's commanding something makes it right.

COMPONENTS OF CHRISTIAN MORALITY

So Christian ethics is a *combination of virtues and principles*. That's another way of saying that God's character and his commands go together. There are moral principles that must be applied and followed, and there are character traits that must be developed, which are evident as moral principles are followed. But Christian ethics is not simply a moral code; it comes out of the framework of a relationship with God. Christian ethics is *an expression of loyalty to God* in gratitude for his goodness to us. Our obedience to the ethical demands of the gospel is a reflection of our relationship with God.

Throughout the Bible, God reassures his people of their secure relationship to him as the context of his commands. For example, in the Mosaic law, both in Exodus and Deuteronomy, God establishes his secure relationship with Israel (through the exodus event in that book and through his getting them to the Promised Land in Deuteronomy) before outlining any of the moral demands on them as a people. Similarly, in the New Testament, in the most theologically oriented epistles, Romans and Ephesians, which spell out the demands of following Jesus, the first half of each book makes clear what God has done for his people (Rom. 1–11; Eph. 1–3), then moves to the moral demands of living consistently with such a gracious God (Rom. 12–16; Eph. 4–6). This relational element to Christian ethics stood in sharp contrast to the legalism of the religious leaders in the time of the NT. Jesus maintained that the leaders' superficial obedience to the law was evidence of their hearts being far from God, since they saw obedience to the law as an end in itself (Mark 7:1–7).

In Christian ethics, obedience to the demands of biblical morality is only a means to an end, not the end itself. The end is a person's relationship to God, and being good is to be seen as an expression of devotion to God. We must not make Christian morality a substitute for a relationship with God, lest we fall back into the error of the first-century religious leaders. This is what the Bible means when it cautions us not to "grieve the Holy Spirit" (Eph. 4:30) or when it describes "godly sorrow" (2 Cor. 7:10) as leading to repentance. Godly sorrow is *sadness that we feel when we hurt someone we love* and is the appropriate emotion when a person falls short of the demands of Christian morality.

So Christian morality is not strictly a moral code but is embedded in a relationship with God. Neither is it something only for individuals. The Bible is clear that the demands of Christian morality are given to *communities* as well. The goal is for the community of God's people to corporately reflect the character of God. This is what the Bible means by the term holiness. It refers to being "set apart" for God's purposes, namely reproducing his character in the world. But holiness is primarily a relational term, and the Bible applies it to communities more often than to individuals. Take, for example, the preface to the Mosaic law in Exodus 19. The goal of the law was to make Israel "a kingdom of priests and *a holy nation*" (Ex. 19:5–6). Similarly, in the NT, the church is to be set apart as God's people, making them distinct from the culture they inhabit. Christian morality is a team sport, not an isolated, individual event.

This community aspect of Christian morality suggests that there is a *social dimension* that is very important. That is, in OT Israel, the law was designed not only to impact the behavior of the community and the individuals in it but also to structure their society, affecting politics, economics, war and peace, and criminal justice. Take, for example, all the various laws that governed how real estate was transacted (Lev. 25). Laws like the Year of Jubilee, the right of redemption, and others were designed to shape economic life in Israel to reflect God's character of justice and compassion. The purpose for the entire civil law was for Israel to reflect a just and properly ordered society, which was to anticipate the social order when the kingdom comes in its fullness after Christ returns.

This is part of what the Messiah was to bring in, foretold in the Prophets. Consider, for example, the first of the Servant Songs of Isaiah (Isa. 42; 49; 50; 53), which portray the Messiah as the Servant of Yahweh. It is true that the final two portraits of the Servant depict his suffering, anticipating the cross. But the first two of these passages outline what will happen at his return. In Isaiah 42:1–4, the Servant will bring justice to the earth (repeated three times), suggesting that he will usher in a just and righteous society which will include the redeemed community. Part of the kingdom fulfillment will be social as well as individual.

This is not to suggest that either today or in the future we would return to what is known as a "theocracy," in which the law of God is automatically the law of the land, as was the case under the Mosaic law in the OT. But the trajectory of the big story of the Bible, and the coming of the kingdom of God in its fullness, indicate that God has a design and a future hope for all of creation, not just for human beings. After all, the entire creation is currently "groaning" for its redemption (Rom. 8:19–22). God is at work redeeming the world, a process which will be completed at Christ's return. This suggests that Christian morality is intended to impact the world and the culture, not only the church, and that as Christian morality is lived out in the world, institutions will be transformed.

This social dimension of Christian morality *has a distinct focus on the poor and the marginalized*. The Bible is full of admonitions to take care of the least among the community. The law set up structures so they were not left hopeless, and the prophets passionately proclaimed justice for the marginalized in the land and called out people who would oppress the poor. Jesus, in the Gospels, maintained that the identifying mark of his coming as Messiah was the way in which the poor were included in his care and in the gospel message (Matt. 11:2–5; Luke 4:14–20). One of the primary distinguishing signs of the early church was the way they cared for the poor among them (Acts 2:42–46; 4:32–35).

The Bible powerfully connects the community's care for the least among us with a person's commitment to God. This goes throughout the Old and New Testaments. For example, Proverbs 14:31 links the treatment of the poor with a person's regard for God. Similarly, the prophets join knowing God rightly with a person's regard for the poor and victimized (Isa. 58:6–8). In perhaps the clearest statement of this connection, Jeremiah puts it this way: "'He defended the cause of the poor and needy, and so all went well. Is that not what it means to know me?' declares the LORD" (Jer. 22:16).

This reflects the NT teaching of both Jesus and the apostles. Jesus makes the remarkable statement, "Whatever you did for one of the least of these brothers and sisters of mine, *you did for me*" (Matt. 25:40). James further connects these when he maintains that "religion that God our Father accepts as pure and faultless is this: to look after orphans and widows in their distress and to keep oneself from being polluted by the world" (James 1:27).

There seems to be something fundamental about following Jesus that involves cultivating a heart for the poor and marginalized. To put this another way, it's difficult to maintain that a person is faithfully following Jesus if characterized by a callous lack of compassion toward the poor and disadvantaged.

We recognize that the demands of Christian morality are difficult and that the bar is high. This challenge highlights one aspect of biblical morality that is unique among the major religions and worldviews. Followers of Jesus are not expected to adhere to Christian morality entirely on their own; they can do it only with *the supernatural assistance of the Holy Spirit.* That is, God's Spirit produces a moral transformation in us that starts with our inmost attitudes and motives and proceeds outward to our actions (Rom 8:13; Gal 5:16–17). The Bible describes the critical character traits as the "fruit of the Spirit," that is, the natural result of the Spirit's activity in someone's life (Gal 5:22–23).

The Bible is clear that simply knowing what is right is no guarantee that a person will do it. In fact, the NT maintains that there is often an inverse relationship between what we want to do and what we actually do. Paul's struggle in Romans 7 brings this out, when he says, "I do not understand what I do. For what I want to do I do not do, but what I hate I do.... For I have the desire to do what is good, but I cannot carry it out. For I do not do the good I want to do, but the evil I do not want to do—this I keep on doing" (Rom 7:15, 18–19). Because of this, Paul affirms that we need the supernatural assistance of the Holy Spirit to do what is right, that simply knowing what is right and wanting to do right are not enough.

The Bible also anticipates that people will fail when it comes to morality, even when assisted by God's Spirit. This is one of the many areas of Christian morality that needs to be accompanied by Christian theology. The good news that Christian theology provides is that *forgiveness and redemption are available to the repentant person in the event of moral failure* (1 John 1:9). The Bible is clear that no moral failure is beyond restoration and no person is so morally flawed that they are outside of reclamation.

So the dominant elements of Christian morality include the following:

- Christian morality consists of a blend of virtues and principles, with its primary source being the character of God.
- Christian morality is set in the context of a relationship with God; it's a relational ethic.
- Christian morality is designed to produce holiness (being set apart) in the community of God's people.
- Christian morality has a significant social dimension; it is designed to impact culture as well as the church.
- This social dimension is focused particularly on the poor, vulnerable, and marginalized among us.
- Christian morality requires the supernatural assistance of the Holy Spirit.
- Christian theology anticipates moral failure and provides for forgiveness and redemption.

NATURAL LAW AND CHRISTIAN MORALITY

So far, we've looked at Christian morality as revealed in the Bible. After all, the Bible is the primary source for knowledge of God's character and commands. But the Bible is not the only source. God communicates morality through his world as well as through his

Word. This is not to suggest that there is anything defective about God's revelation of morality in his Word. But the Bible is clear that everyone is accountable for being moral, regardless of his or her access to God's Word. For example, in the Old Testament, the nations outside Israel were just as accountable as Israel was to the moral demands of the Mosaic law. In the oracles of judgment against the nations (Isa. 13–27; Jer. 46–51; Ezek. 25–32), the prophets condemned the nations for most of the same things for which they condemned Israel—violence, oppression of the poor, and idolatry. This suggests that the nations were equally as accountable as Israel was to the law. Whether they had access to the law was irrelevant to their accountability. The only way this can be fair is if they had access to those moral standards in some other way that was outside the written Mosaic law.

Remember the moral sense that was discussed in chapter 1? The idea of the law "written on our hearts" is a good example of God revealing morality outside the pages of the Bible. In fact, the point of that passage (Rom. 2:14–15) is that everyone, regardless of his or her access to the law, is accountable to it. What keeps that from being cosmically unfair is that all human beings have the moral law of God imprinted on them, and as a result, no one can claim an exemption from accountability.

The Bible is clear that God has embedded his wisdom in the world. Proverbs 8, in which wisdom is personified, indicates that from the beginning God has engraved his wisdom, including his moral wisdom, into his creation. Wisdom is described as being there as the world was being formed (Prov. 8:22–31). What follows next brings out the moral implications of this. Proverbs 8:32–36 reads,

> Now then, my children, listen to me [Wisdom];
>> blessed are those who keep my [Wisdom's] ways.
> Listen to my instruction and be wise;
>> do not disregard it.
> Blessed are those who listen to me,
>> watching daily at my doors,

> waiting at my doorway.
> For those who find me find life
> and receive favor from the LORD.
> But those who fail to find me harm themselves;
> all who hate me love death.

Remember, everywhere the first person pronoun (me, my) is used, it is referring to God's wisdom embedded in his world. Notice the moral instruction that comes out of this. In fact, it's parallel to other parts of the Bible that describe the Mosaic law, which was engraved on tablets in the same way God's law was engraved into his world. Blessing and life come from paying attention to God's wisdom as revealed in his world.

A specific example of this wisdom is found in Proverbs 6:6–11, where the sage observes the diligence and forethought of the ant and draws a moral conclusion about diligence and laziness. Similarly, Proverbs 24:30–34 draws the identical conclusion, repeated verbatim, from observation of a lazy person and the consequences of laziness. Thus observations drawn from the physical and interpersonal worlds are some of the sources for gleaning God's natural wisdom and drawing appropriate moral conclusions.

Of course, the revelation in Scripture has a clarity that natural law does not, and the Bible speaks to much more than morality, including the important matters of salvation and eternity. But natural law is important in that it provides a bridge that can connect Christian morality to an increasingly secular culture. Without something like natural law, it is difficult to say anything about morality to the culture that considers an appeal to the Bible to be a nonstarter. Being able to appeal to moral principles and virtues that are held in common regardless of one's worldview is a great help in bringing Christian morality to bear on issues facing the culture, without explicit reliance on the Bible. The Bible is fully adequate as a source of moral authority, but it is not the only source of moral knowledge that comes from God.

MORAL CONFLICTS

At times, in a fallen, broken world, biblical principles and God's commands conflict. For example, during World War II, when Corrie ten Boom gave sanctuary to Jews in her native country of the Netherlands, the authorities often asked her if she was hiding Jews in her home. If she told the truth, the Jews would have been taken to extermination camps. But if she lied, they would have been saved. Here she was faced with a genuine moral dilemma, or a conflict of commands. She had a moral duty to tell the truth, but she was also responsible for saving life when it was in her power to do so.

Or consider the example of Rahab in Joshua 2. Here Rahab the prostitute was commended for her faith in sheltering the Israelite spies sent out on a reconnaissance mission to the Promised Land. The authorities directly asked her if she knew the location of any Israelite spies. Not only did she tell the authorities that she did not know where the spies were, but she also sent them in the wrong direction when she was actually hiding the spies on her roof. She is commended for the entire episode, of which the deception was an integral part, by her inclusion in the "faith hall of fame" in Hebrews 11. How should we think about these kinds of scenarios that involve conflicts of biblical commands and moral principles?

One way to think about this is to maintain that no conflict actually faces the believer. Theologically, it goes something like this: Since an infallible God inspired his inerrant Word, no such conflict of commands is possible. The way out of these "dilemmas" would be to appeal to God's providence to somehow open an opportunity where both commands could be fulfilled. According to this view, Corrie ten Boom should have told the truth and trusted God to work out his will for the Jews she was hiding.

A second way to think about these situations is to admit that real moral conflicts do exist, but sin is still sin, even when a person is faced with competing obligations. Advocates of this view hold that because we live in a fallen world, real moral conflicts can and do occur, and perhaps we should be surprised that they do not occur more frequently. God's law is absolute, moral conflicts are inevitable in a fallen world, and people have the duty to do the lesser evil. But it is still evil, for which forgiveness is available for the Christian.

This is the way that the well-known German pastor Dietrich Bonhoeffer thought about the moral dilemma he faced during WWII. He was a pacifist but also felt a duty to stop Hitler's tyranny, and thus he participated in the plot to kill Hitler. He believed he had to choose the lesser of two evils facing him. From this framework, one can conclude that Corrie ten Boom should have lied to protect the Jews, the lie being the lesser of two evils facing her. Then she should have immediately repented and asked God for forgiveness for lying. The problem often raised against this view is that having a duty to sin in certain situations is morally problematic. It is hard to imagine that a person can be morally culpable for something that could not be avoided and about which the person had no choice.

A third way to think about this is close to the previous one. Like the second view, this framework holds that moral conflicts are real because of life in a fallen world. However, the option chosen is not evil, and it is not correct to say that the person chose the "lesser evil." The choice is a morally justifiable option, not sin, and thus there is no need for repentance. This view attempts to combine the nature of God's commands, the reality of life in a fallen world, and a proper understanding of moral accountability. Therefore in this view, Corrie ten Boom should have lied to protect the Jews she was harboring, and she would have been morally justified in lying to protect their lives.

CONCLUSION

This short sketch of the elements of Christian morality has focused on some of the critical components of morality in a Christian world-view. We've suggested that Christian morality is a blend of virtues and principles, with the character of God as the ultimate source.

Some of the distinct elements of Christian morality include the relational, social, and community emphasis, with a special obligation to care for the least among us. Further, Christian morality requires the divine assistance of the Holy Spirit and ample doses of forgiveness and redemption. God communicates these moral demands through his Word and his world, as the discussion of natural law maintains. Periodically, as a result of living in a fallen world, we face genuine moral conflicts in which principles are opposed; these necessitate weighting principles to come up with a morally justifiable course of action.

Christian morality is an *objective morality*, meaning that its content is true regardless of how one feels about it. Further, as the discussion of natural law suggested, since everyone has access to God's moral demands regardless of their contact with the Bible, all are accountable. This means that Christian morality is a *universal morality*, applicable to all cultures, though the specific way in which particular principles and virtues are applied may vary widely from culture to culture. It is a *transcendent morality*, since it comes from God and is not fundamentally a human creation. It is discovered by human beings, not created by them. Because of these elements, we can say that Christian morality is not a matter of a person's opinion but is made up of moral facts that constitute knowledge about the moral fabric of the world.

Review Questions

1. What is the ultimate source for Christian morality?
2. What are main components of Christian morality?
3. What is natural law, and how is it part of Christian morality?
4. How do you resolve moral conflicts such as the ones that Corrie ten Boom or Rahab faced?

For Further Reading

Budziszewski, J. *What We Can't Not Know: A Guide.* Dallas: Spence, 2003.

Hollinger, Dennis P. *Choosing the Good: Christian Ethics in a Complex World.* Grand Rapids: Baker, 2002.

CHAPTER 3

CULTURAL VIEWS OF MORALITY

Why can't we make up our own
moral rules for ourselves?

Recently, I was invited to speak to a group of public high school students during their lunch hour on the subject of relativism and ethics. It turned out to be a lively time, with lots of interaction and people feeling the freedom to say whatever was on their minds. In the middle of the session, one of the students, who had apparently been holding back, blurted out, "I don't get what's so complicated about this. We should all be able to make our moral rules for ourselves!"

I commented briefly, acknowledging the remark, but also noticed that the person had a brand new iPhone in plain view on her desk. As I went on to the next point, I casually picked up her phone and put it in my pocket. She didn't say anything at the time, but at the end of the session, as I got ready to leave, she asked, "Aren't you going to give me my iPhone back?" I replied, "No, I'm not." When she asked why, I said, "Well, you said that we should all be able to make up our own moral rules for ourselves. My moral rules are that those who are older, wiser, and more experienced are entitled to the stuff of those who are younger and less experienced."

She didn't know quite what to say in response, since I had used her view of morality against her. I then pointed out that although it may sound good to think of everyone making up their own morality for themselves, it's hard to live consistently in such a system. She gave up her view pretty quickly when she was victimized by my injustice. She became a quite rigid absolutist when it came to the principle of private property!

In our culture today, morality is widely viewed as a matter of subjective opinion, much like someone's taste in ice cream or preference for vacation places. Yet we tend to reserve our most passionate debates for those issues that have moral implications, suggesting that we don't actually view them as mere matters of opinion. Otherwise, we wouldn't work so hard to defend our views, not to mention to change people's minds.

We realize how difficult it would be to live in a culture in which all moral issues were regarded as matters of opinion, recognizing that if we all made up our own moral rules for ourselves, it wouldn't be long before chaos ensued, since we would have no basis for resolving moral conflicts between individuals or communities. Thankfully, like the student whose iPhone I took (and returned!), most people give up this idea that morality is only a matter of opinion once they become a victim of some kind of injustice. They end up realizing that some moral values, regardless of how we personally view them, are critical if society is to function peacefully. The foundation on which those are based—that's the real point of debate culturally.

Let's look more carefully at how people in our culture generally think about morality. As we do this, and by way of contrast, keep in mind what a Christian ethic looks like from our discussion in chapter 2. We will briefly outline the major ways in which people regard morality today, with examples of each style of moral reasoning. We are asking here not only what a person's position is on a particular issue but also, more importantly, on what basis do they come to their view of right and wrong.

DEONTOLOGICAL ETHICS

A first, and common, way to look at morality is what is called a *deontological* view of right and wrong. This way of viewing morality suggests that things are right or wrong based on adherence to certain moral *principles*. That is, in this view, things are intrinsically right or wrong, and neither the context nor the consequences matter. Actions are wrong if they violate moral principles, or values, and are right if they uphold them or are consistent with them.

A deontological view does not necessarily make one a moral absolutist, since one can be what is called a *prima facie* deontologist. Prima facie is a Latin term meaning "at first face," or what we commonly refer to as "at first glance." When applied to principle-based morality, it means that the principles are generally applicable but can have periodic exceptions, particularly when they come into conflict with other important moral principles. Take the example, cited in chapter 2, of Corrie ten Boom lying to the Nazis in order to protect innocent life. We argued that she was justified in doing so. That means we are viewing the principle of truth telling as a prima facie principle—normally the case but with periodic exceptions. Consider, for example, other exceptions to the principle of truth telling, such as undercover police work, that involve deception about one's identity. We generally take this type of activity as an exception to the general rule that obligates people to tell the truth.

Deontological forms of moral reasoning raise the question, where do these principles come from? Most "religions of the book," including Islam, Judaism, and Christianity, are heavily deontological, since they rely on the values that come out of the commands and precepts in their respective scriptures. Other versions of deontological reasoning include a natural law approach, which insists that God has embedded his moral values in his world and given human beings the necessary tools to discover them, apart from any religious book. This form of deontology would be more characteristic of Roman Catholicism. Principles in government documents such as the US Constitution or the UN Charter on Human Rights are often seen as examples of natural law deontology. They are perceived as virtually self-evident moral values which are part of a reservoir of shared values that are widely recognized.

To be fair, though there may be considerable consensus about these values, there is also considerable debate over the source. In addition, there are types of deontological ethics that do not rely on religious views at all. For example, the deontological system of the eighteenth-century philosopher Immanuel Kant derived moral principles based on reason alone, resulting in what is known as the categorical imperative.

Think about the occasions in which you might see a deontological view of morality in use. What issues are debated on deontological grounds? Take, for example, the issue of abortion. Pro-life advocates commonly refer to the principle of the sanctity of life to defend the right to life of the unborn. Of course, they are making the argument that the unborn are persons entitled to that right. They also invoke the principle, coming from the Bible, of the duty to protect the most vulnerable among us, which surely includes the unborn. On the other hand, pro-choice advocates argue from the principle of bodily integrity, which gives someone the right over their own body. Of course, they are assuming that the fetus is part of the woman's body, over which she has control.

Both assumptions—that of the personhood of the unborn and that of the fetus being part of the woman's body—should not obscure the fact that both sides in the debate are invoking moral principles to make their case. Some abortion advocates are even conceding the personhood of the unborn and weighting the principle of bodily integrity more heavily than the sanctity of the life of the unborn. All this comes from within a deontological approach to the issue.

A similar approach is taken to the heavily debated issue of physician-assisted suicide (PAS). Opponents of PAS appeal to the same principles as do pro-life advocates. They argue that the sanctity of life mandates against suicide, either assisted or not. They further argue that the principle of protecting the vulnerable applies to the elderly, who are susceptible to coercion and often unable to speak for themselves. Proponents of PAS argue in a way similar to that of pro-choice advocates, maintaining a right of bodily integrity—the right to do with one's own body as one chooses. In addition, they appeal to a principle of personal autonomy, that people should have the right to determine the timing and manner of their deaths.

Another issue debated on deontological grounds is the death penalty, with proponents pointing to the principle of justice (life for life) and opponents pointing to the sanctity of life, suggesting that the taking of life is not a human prerogative. Other examples of a deontological basis for morality include: sexual assault, considered wrong because it's an assault on a woman's dignity, autonomy, and bodily integrity; adultery, judged to be wrong because it violates the principle of promise keeping to one's spouse; and fraud in business, deemed wrong because it violates the principle of truth telling and covenant keeping.

Deontological reasoning appeals to many people's deepest intuitions about moral matters, and if pushed hard enough, many people will default to deontological arguments to defend their views. Many people hold that some things are "just plain wrong." They may not be able to articulate the principle that makes it plain wrong, but what they often mean is that there's something intrinsic to the action that makes it almost self-evidently wrong. For example, they would hold that sexual assault is self-evidently wrong, and it doesn't matter what the consequences are or in what context it takes place (in fact, even mentioning the calculus of consequences with sexual assault is often seen as offensive). As my colleague William Lane Craig pointed out, "Anyone who thinks sexual assault is okay needs a therapist, not an argument!"

However, this does not mean that deontological forms of reasoning don't have shortcomings too. It is a challenge to resolve moral dilemmas on strictly deontological grounds when the principles conflict, though, as we will see in chapter 4, there is a way to weight competing principles and avoid a stalemate. In addition, the principles may not resolve the issue, or they may be so general that there may be several valid ways of applying them to the situation at hand, perhaps producing more debate rather than resolving it.

Further, principles can be applied rigidly and legalistically, leading to a moral system resembling that of the religious leaders so roundly condemned by Jesus.

TELEOLOGICAL/UTILITARIAN ETHICS

A second common way of looking at morality is just the opposite of a deontological view. This way of moral reasoning is known as *teleological* reasoning. In this system, the outcome is what determines right and wrong. Unlike deontological reasoning, teleology affirms that nothing is intrinsically right or wrong, since it depends on the consequences produced by the action. The most common form of teleological reasoning is known as *utilitarianism*, the moral theory popularized by John Stuart Mill in the mid-1800s. The shorthand version of utilitarianism is that morality is determined by *the greatest good for the greatest number*. That is, the action that produces the greatest balance of benefits over harms is the moral thing to do. It is, in essence, a moral form of cost-benefit analysis.

Examples of this abound in the world of public policy, particularly given that religious principles and virtues are, in effect, ruled out of the discussion. Take the debate over the use of embryonic stem cells for research and treatment. The most compelling argument in favor of using those stem cells is the numbers of potential patients who could be helped by treatments developed by means of them. In addition, much of the moral discussion around reproductive technologies is dominated by the outcome that all infertile couples desperately desire—a healthy baby. On a utilitarian basis, the ends are all that matter. Not only do they justify the means, but the means are not subject to much scrutiny.

Utilitarian arguments contribute to the principled debates over issues mentioned earlier, such as abortion and assisted suicide. One of the arguments for the pro-choice side in the debate over abortion has to do with what consequences would presumably result if the law restricted access to abortion services. Proponents of that view allege that society would go backward to the days before abortion was legalized, when women were forced to go to less-qualified physicians in less medically appropriate facilities. Pro-life advocates have their utilitarian argument too. They insist that liberal abortion laws produce callousness to life, which results in a trend toward infanticide and a cheapening of respect for life at the end of life.

Similarly, the dispute over physician-assisted suicide has its utilitarian side. Proponents of PAS argue that allowing it produces good all around. The patient dies peacefully and quietly without his or her death being drawn out, the family is able to grieve and get on with their lives, and considerable money is saved that would have gone into expensive end-of-life care. On the other hand, opponents of PAS argue that legalizing it produces an unwanted consequence, that what starts out as fully voluntary assistance eventually becomes nonvoluntary, as frail and vulnerable elderly men and women are coerced into agreeing to PAS.

Utilitarian reasoning is often used to either justify or condemn actions that can be viewed on deontological grounds. For example, according to the utilitarian, sexual assault is wrong because of the real, tangible harm it causes to the person assaulted. Adultery is wrong because of the damage it causes to families, often leading to marriages breaking up and problems for the children. Fraud is wrong because of the financial losses it brings to the victim(s).

For the utilitarian, what makes something wrong is the calculus of harms over benefits. Conversely, telling the truth would be right because it makes meaningful communication possible, and trustworthiness is right because of the good effect it has on relationships. The person who holds to a deontological system, particularly a religiously based one, would argue that of course, this is precisely what we would expect, that the behavior which adheres to principles also produces the best set of consequences for the greatest number of people. This may be the reason why the Bible sometimes appeals to consequences as a supplement to the commands of the law. For example, the proverbs of the OT are overwhelmingly based on the good consequences of wisdom and good character and the harmful consequences of being unwise and lacking character.

There are two somewhat different forms of utilitarianism, *act utilitarianism* and *rule utilitarianism*. The former evaluates the utility of individual actions, and the latter provides moral rules based on a predictable track record of consequences. For example, sexual assault would be judged to be always wrong by the rule utilitarian because there are many foreseeable harms that sexual assault victims have in common. Further, it is clear that with every sexual assault, there is an expected calculus of harms over benefits. Rule utilitarianism may produce the same kind of moral absolutes as deontological forms of reasoning, but from an entirely different basis.

From its inception, utilitarianism has had considerable appeal due to its basing morality on grounds other than religious views. That was the attraction to Mill, who explicitly wanted an ethic that was not dependent on religious worldviews and thus would not be the source of religious conflict and violence. This reflects its current appeal for use in public policy debates, avoiding what is widely perceived as contentious use of religiously based arguments and providing a means of argument that is open to everyone regardless of worldview commitments. In the US, public policy makers are very sensitive to violating the separation of church and state and are very skeptical about using religiously based reasoning. Utilitarian arguments are seen as something everyone can embrace irrespective of their basic philosophy of life and is thus perceived as an effective means of resolving public policy disputes.

Despite its appeal, utilitarianism has some significant inadequacies. One is that to be a good utilitarian, it helps to be omniscient! That is, to assess fully the consequences of any action requires the ability to see into the future. The reality is that no one can completely know what the eventual consequences of any action will be, and as a result, no one can ever come to a place where a decision can be made, since the jury is always out on the final calculus of consequences.

A further problem with the utilitarian mode of reasoning comes with the question, what makes a good outcome so good? or, what makes a bad outcome so bad? For example, in the case of murder, what makes the loss of the victim's life such a bad thing? It could be the lost opportunities for a positive contribution, but we don't know what the future of that person would have looked like. Rather what makes it such a bad outcome is that we consider that person's life a sacred thing. That is, what tells us something is a bad or good outcome is a prior commitment to some sort of principle that the utilitarian is smuggling into the argument.

A final problem with utilitarian reasoning is that the maxim "The greatest good for the greatest number," by definition, makes it difficult to protect the rights and interests of minorities. For example, it is not difficult to make a utilitarian argument that slavery produced the greatest balance of benefits over harms. But most people, when they evaluate slavery, would say that the calculus of benefits and harms is irrelevant to the intrinsic wrongs that were done to slaves. In fact, most people might find the notion that slavery could have any benefits to be very offensive, given the inherent wrong done to slaves during that time.

ETHICAL EGOISM

A third type of ethical reasoning is known as *ethical egoism*. This is the view that what is in a person's *self-interest* is what determines right and wrong. Don't confuse this with selfishness or narcissism. Ethical egoism is not a license to do whatever you want to do. Egoism and egotism are not the same thing. Rather ethical egoism is the system in which the moral thing to do is that which advances one's self-interest.

The ethical egoist argues that a person's moral duty is only to his or her own self-interest. This view was first widely articulated by the enlightenment philosopher Thomas Hobbes and has been popularized more recently by the writer Ayn Rand. This is often the moral view of political libertarians like Rand, who frequently apply it to the workings of the "invisible hand" of the free market, which maximizes the general welfare as everyone pursues his or her self-interest. It is commonly associated with a view of human nature known as *psychological egoism*, the view that human beings are capable only of acting in their self-interest and that any suggestion of altruism is only masking one's deepest, subconscious commitment to self-interest.

Of course, the converse of this—that in our deepest subconscious, human beings are entirely other-centered—could also be true, since neither view can be verified. In addition, one can raise the question of why ethical egoism is necessary if psychological egoism is true. Why it is crucial to have a moral system tell me I ought to do things that are in my self-interest, when my view of human nature tells me I'm incapable of doing otherwise?

To clarify how ethical egoism works, consider these examples of moral decisions being made on egoistic grounds. Observe the issue of abortion and a college student with an unwanted pregnancy. One of the most common justifications for ending that pregnancy is that "having this baby will ruin *my life*!" For many young women facing this situation, the appeal to egoism is all the rationale they need to justify having an abortion. For the ethical egoist, other moral considerations, such as the moral status of the unborn, are irrelevant to the woman's self-interest. However, on egoistic grounds, a good case could be made for keeping the pregnancy and putting the baby up for adoption, avoiding the long-term regret and depression that often result from having the abortion.

Or consider the case of assisted suicide. You could argue that it's in your self-interest to go through with assisted suicide, that it prevents suffering, gives you control over your life and death, and allows you to use your financial resources in ways other than paying doctors and hospitals. However, you could also maintain that egoism would suggest you die naturally, so you would have your family around you, ushering you up to the doorstep to eternity, so you would not be vulnerable to coercion to accept PAS, and so you would benefit from additional time with friends and family.

Other examples of the use of egoism include "whistleblowers." When a person thinks his or her company is involved in illegal or immoral activity, they are often tempted to expose the wrongdoing by blowing the whistle on the organization. In most cases, they choose not to do so, primarily because whistleblowers are often fired, blackballed by their industries, and labeled as troublemakers. In other words, blowing the whistle is rarely in a person's self-interest, and in a desire to protect their jobs and livelihood, potential whistleblowers often turn a blind eye to the wrongdoing and reluctantly justify doing so on egoistic grounds.

Or take physicians who are treating patients in end-of-life situations and are dealing with families who want their loved ones to continue with all aggressive treatments up to the end, although the doctor knows that these treatments are either futile or harmful to the patients. The physician knows that families will threaten to sue them if they don't follow their wishes, and physicians are very reluctant to risk a lawsuit, given the major inconvenience, financial repercussions, and reputational harm that all come from being sued. This is why it's not uncommon for doctors to administer treatments they strongly suspect are futile or harmful in order to avoid being taken to court, and they justify it on egoistic grounds.

As a moral system, egoism, though it clearly has appeal, has some serious shortcomings. It is naive to assume that in a community attempting to live peacefully together, self-interests won't ever conflict. It's inevitable that they will, given the inherent self-centeredness of human beings. Yet egoism can only assert the primacy of self-interest in the face of these conflicts. It has no resources for resolving them, except for using power to enforce one person's self-interest over another's. In addition, it is an arbitrary ethical system. It divides people into two groups and says that the interests of one group count more than the interests of the other. Both anti-Semitism and racism illustrate this.

Advocates of those ideologies insist that the interests of their group count more than the interests of Jews or any other race different from their own. In general, treating groups differently is justifiable if there are relevant differences between the groups. An anti-Semite or racist cannot point consistently to any criteria that justify anti-Semitism or racism. Egoism advocates that we divide the world into two groups—myself and the rest of the world—and that we regard the interests of the first group as more important than those of the second. But why I should be in such a privileged category is never addressed.

This critique of egoism is not to say that the Bible has no place for self-interest. This is part of the false dichotomy that the egoist creates in order to make the system appealing. It is simply not true that self-interest and altruism cannot coexist. Though it is true that following Jesus involves denying oneself, taking up one's cross, and following him (Mark 8:34–35), the Bible also calls people to balance self-interest with a concern for the interests of others (Phil. 2:4). In addition, the Bible mandates that individuals pursue their self-interest so they can take care of their financial needs and those of their dependents, without being dependent on the community (1 Tim. 5:8; 2 Thess. 3:10). The Bible even uses the national self-interest of Israel as a motive for obeying the Mosaic law. The covenant blessings and curses (Deut. 27–30) are an appeal to Israel's wish to prosper and have peace in the Promised Land. Obedience to the law was partially based on their desire that it go well for them in the land, that is, on their recognition that it was in their interest to follow the law.

RELATIVISM

Relativism is perhaps the dominant view of morality in the culture of the West today. It is the view that morality is relative to one's culture and community, and as a result there are no moral absolutes that transcend time and culture. The maxim "When in Rome, do as the Romans do" can be changed to "When in Rome, it's morally justifiable to do as the Romans do." That is, morality is determined by the consensus of the culture you are in. This is why in so many parts of Western culture, it is out of fashion to criticize other cultures or assert that one culture is morally superior or inferior to another.

Moral relativism became popular as a result of the findings of cultural anthropologists around the end of the nineteenth century and the beginning of the twentieth century. These anthropologists observed that different cultures had widely varying moral codes and concepts of right and wrong. What is often forgotten is their observation of how much morality the different cultures also had in common. But from this diversity they saw, the anthropologists concluded that it's not possible to believe in moral absolutes that transcend culture.

One of the byproducts of the current emphasis on cultural diversity is a renewal of cultural relativism, which was inevitable, given the makeup of cultures around the world. It's one thing to appreciate the customs of a culture—its dress, cuisine, artistic expressions, and language. But the most important part of any culture, that which defines it, is its *values.* The way a culture thinks about right and wrong is central to its identity. Therefore to genuinely appreciate diversity, one has to appreciate diverse values, and to do so without assessment is essentially accepting cultural relativism in morality. It's also true that the postmodern skepticism about truth and moral absolutes has also contributed to the renewal of relativism, especially at the popular level.

Relativism also exists at an individual level, in what is known as moral subjectivism—or cultural relativism for a culture of one person, namely, the individual. Here morality is determined by a person's subjective tastes and preferences and is captured by the maxim "We make up our own moral rules for ourselves." Moral subjectivism tells us that morality is a matter of opinion, analogous to someone's taste in ice cream. This view is widely, though inconsistently, held in much of Western culture today.

To be clear on this, let's be sure to distinguish between things that are subjective and their opposite, things that are objective.

Subjective means that how a person feels about something determines its truth. By contrast, objective means that how a person feels about something is irrelevant to its truth. For example, how you feel about the law of gravity when you're getting ready to jump out of an airplane is simply not relevant to the fact that if you don't have a parachute, you will die from the effects of gravity. Conversely, how you feel about which flavor of ice cream tastes best is precisely what determines which is the best—to you.

An interesting exercise to do with someone who maintains that morality is subjective is to ask them to differentiate between objective and subjective statements. For example, "Regular Coke has more calories than Diet Coke" is an objective statement that can be verified, but "Regular Coke tastes better than Diet Coke" is a subjective one, a matter of opinion only. Then ask them about a moral issue, whether it's objective or subjective. Take the example "Abortion, except to save the life of the mother, is morally wrong." Chances are, they will answer that it is a subjective statement, just a matter of opinion. But that may be because the issue of abortion is so debated throughout the culture.

So take another moral statement, "Human trafficking is morally wrong." Here you might get a different answer, because virtually everyone agrees that human trafficking is wrong. I suspect most people would say that someone who thinks human trafficking is acceptable doesn't simply have a different opinion. We would say that they are wrong.

Substitute any number of other examples, and you would get the same answer. Someone who holds that racial discrimination is acceptable doesn't just hold a contrary view. We would say that they are wrong. The same would hold true for sexual assault or the murder of innocent children. This suggests that morality is more objective than subjective, that it is more than simply a matter of opinion.

Culturally, moral statements have been relegated to matters of subjective belief. But the Bible holds that morality is objective and that the statements are matters of fact and knowledge. It is true that they cannot be verified empirically, like facts in the sciences. But the view that "what counts for knowledge are those matters that are empirically verifiable" is itself not empirically verifiable. Just as we can know history, which is verified differently, we can also know morality, because of its ultimate source in God's character, expressed in his Word and his world.

The many passionate moral debates we have at present are an indication that morality is something we consider to be objective. The reason why we try so hard to persuade others in moral discussion is that we believe that what we hold to be true is objectively the case. We are trying to persuade someone of what we think is right. Otherwise, why would we argue so passionately about something that is only a matter of subjective opinion? We don't argue with each other about flavors of ice cream, the most beautiful vacation spots on earth, or other matters of subjective opinion. Of course, often the reason why we disagree on moral matters is that what is morally right is not always clear, and sometimes a good argument is possible for more than one position. Further, it may be that we hold principles and virtues in common, but the application looks a bit different in different cultures.

To be sure, there is moral disagreement, but our Christian ethic of natural law suggests that there also is a reservoir of shared values that transcends culture. Look at all the moral commonalities between cultures. As C. S. Lewis pointed out in *The Abolition of Man*, cultures throughout the history of civilization have held many values in common, such as the sanctity of life, the importance of marriage and family, and the mandate to tell the truth.

Seeing morality as strictly a matter of opinion, believing that we make up our own moral rules for ourselves, is a difficult view of morality with which to live consistently. Think back to the beginning of this chapter, with the young woman whose iPhone I pocketed during my lecture on relativism. Remember how she readily gave up her relativism once she became a victim of injustice? Most people reject the notion that we make up morality for ourselves when they are on the receiving end of a clear injustice. They don't say that they have merely been treated differently. Rather, they say they have been *wronged*.

CONCLUSION

This very brief sketch of some of the ways morality is viewed culturally is important for identifying the ways most people think about right and wrong. To be sure, some of these modes of moral reasoning have elements in common with a Christian ethic. Christian ethics is heavily principle-oriented and has a considerable commonality with deontological ethics. Of course, Christian ethics also has a significant component of virtue, which takes the origin of morality back to God's character and suggests that morality is more than simply doing the right thing; it also involves *being the right kind of person*. In addition, there is a place for considering consequences in Christian ethics, though as a supplement to principles and virtues, not in place of them. They are the caboose of the train, not the engine that drives it. Further, there is a place for self-interest, but not as the primary basis for morality, and balanced by altruism and love of neighbor.

The discussion in this chapter, hopefully, will help to identify the way others think about morality in general. This is equally important to recognizing someone's position on a particular issue. Often we focus on what position someone holds on a specific moral issue. That's important, but it's also critical to identify how they think about right and wrong more generally and how they justify their position. What a person believes makes something right or wrong is often very revealing about their overall view of morality. To be sharp in ethics involves being able to identify both a person's position and the way they are reasoning morally about it.

Review Questions

1. How would you answer the question posed at the beginning of the chapter: "Why can't we make up our own moral rules for ourselves?"

2. Give an example of each of the ethical systems introduced in this chapter: deontological, utilitarianism, egoism, and relativism.

3. How would you defend the idea that morality is objective?

For Further Reading

Rae, Scott B. *Doing the Right Thing: Making Moral Choices in a World Full of Options.* Grand Rapids: Zondervan, 2013.

Wilkens, Steve. *Beyond Bumper Sticker Ethics: An Introduction to Theories of Right and Wrong,* 2nd ed. Downers Grove, Ill.: InterVarsity Press, 2010.

CHAPTER 4

MAKING ETHICAL DECISIONS

When I'm in a moral dilemma, what do I do?

Imagine being in the middle of the following scenario at your workplace. You are a group manager in your company, with around twenty people who report to you. Your company is publicly traded, not privately owned. There are many rumors going around the company that layoffs are coming because of a slowdown in business, making the employees in your group feel anxious and worried and unsure of their job prospects should they be let go. You know these rumors are true.

Only a few top executives and the group managers know the names of the people who will be laid off, and the company has a policy of strict confidentiality when it comes to who is on the layoff list. The reason for this is that when word leaked out in the past, some of the affected employees left before their termination date, leaving the company in a difficult situation in terms of finishing jobs that needed to be done. In addition, some employees, out of anger and a desire to strike back at the company, resorted to sabotage of company equipment, especially their computers. Normally, keeping confidentiality about these matters is not a problem. But here it raises an ethical issue for you, because your good friend, John, is on the layoff list.

John is a computer systems analyst who has been with the company for the past several years and whose expertise is important for his current project. If he were to leave early, it would be problematic for the project he's working on, causing delays and perhaps jeopardizing future contracts with this client.

But John is also your good friend. The two of you have become close friends over the years, in part because you are both in a similar stage of life, with children roughly the same ages. John and his wife are about to have their fourth child in the next few months. At one of the kids' soccer games, John mentions that he's received a job offer from another company, but he says he would rather stay in his present job because the pay is better and the commute is much shorter. He tells you he tried to get them to give him more time to make a decision, at least until the layoffs are made public, but the company who offered him the job needs to know before then.

John asks you, "Do you think I should take this position?" You remain silent because of your obligation to your company. He knows you are bound by confidentiality but says anyway, "I know you can't say anything directly about the layoffs, but am I safe to assume that your nonresponse is good news for me? Given our relationship over the years, you would probably warn me in a roundabout way if I were being laid off, right? Besides, by giving me some indication, you would be doing much more good than harm. No one gets hurt if you let me know. Think of what I stand to lose if you don't tell me."

Your friend John has put you in quite a dilemma. You're caught between two difficult choices—to tell him and violate your company's policy about confidentiality, or not to tell him and risk your friend passing up on a job he should take, given that he is about to be laid off. What do you do? Perhaps more important, how do you decide what to do?

Often in situations like these, people just trust their gut. They do what their intuition tells them to do, without much critical thinking about it. To be sure, in a lot of cases you don't have time to engage in a decision-making process, since you must decide on the spot. But many moral decisions are not like that. You do have time to consider more thoughtfully what to do. In those situations, the decision-making model presented in this chapter may be helpful. Even in those scenarios that require snap decisions, using this model can be beneficial in retrospect, particularly if they are situations that may arise again in the future. It can be a useful tool to help individuals or groups debrief after facing an ethical dilemma.

A MODEL FOR MAKING ETHICAL DECISIONS

This is a procedure that can be followed in private reflection and decision making or can be used to facilitate group discussion and deliberation on ethical issues. It is not a formula that automatically generates the right decision. Rather it is a process that insures that all the important questions are asked and all the bases are covered. It can be used by people with a wide variety of worldviews—an important factor, given the diversity of our workplaces today. It is not a distinctly Christian model, though it is consistent with the Bible, since it holds principles and virtues in a prominent position. Thus you will notice that it is heavily deontological and virtue oriented, with a consideration of consequences playing a supporting role.

What makes many moral dilemmas so difficult is that the Bible does not always address an issue directly, if it addresses that issue at all. General biblical virtues and principles are relevant and should be applied to the issue being discussed. However, there is often disagreement about which biblical principles and virtues are applicable and how they apply to the situation at hand. Further, it may be that the principles/virtues conflict in any given scenario. These tend to be some of the most difficult ethical dilemmas, because they involve making choices and weighting the principles/virtues that have a bearing on the case.

Appeal to principles and virtues alone will not necessarily resolve any particular dilemma. Of course, appealing to the Bible, either to a specific text or to more general principles, can conclusively resolve many moral questions, but there are other cases in which it's more challenging to do that. Thankfully, many areas in ethics are clear and straightforward, and we don't face ethical dilemmas every day. But when we do, it's helpful to have a procedure to follow that is consistent with our worldview.

Clearly, the place to start is recognizing an ethical dilemma. If you ask someone to tell you how he or she would know if they were facing an ethical dilemma, I suspect you would get a "deer in the headlights" look! So here's the definition of an ethical dilemma: *a conflict between two or more principle/virtue-driven interests.* To be more specific, you must identify the parties who have an interest in the case, determine their interests, and most important, define the moral principles and/or virtues that underlie their interests. If you cannot point out the principles/virtues in their interests, then it's likely that you have some other kind of dilemma, perhaps a strategic one but not an ethical dilemma. One way to clarify this is to ask yourself, "If one party's interests were ignored, what moral principle or virtue would be violated?"

Be sure to distinguish between an ethical dilemma and a temptation; a temptation does not have another competing principle/virtue but is normally a conflict between a moral principle/virtue and a person's self-interest. So once you know you are facing an ethical dilemma, how do you proceed?

I am indebted to Dr. William W. May for this model.

1. Gather the Facts

This section is for clarifying two main things: what do we know? and what do we need to know? Since these decisions are often being made in real time, we have time to ask questions and clarify things and bring to light facts that need uncovering. Of course, in utilizing this model in retrospect, the question, what do we need to know? can't be answered, but in a debriefing discussion after the fact, it's possible to ask, what would have been helpful to know at the time that we didn't?

2. Identify the Ethical Issue

Remember, an ethical dilemma is defined as a conflict between two or more principle/virtue-driven interests. Pinpointing the conflict is critical in this step. Be careful here; it's not the conflict between competing alternatives but the conflict between competing principles/virtues that counts. Don't confuse competing choices with the ethical issue. Remember that people in these discussions can become very passionate about their views, since their views are based on deeply held moral values.

3. What Additional Principles/Virtues Have a Bearing on the Case?

Usually, once the competing interests and their underlying principles/virtues are clear, those moral principles and virtues are not the only ones that are relevant to the issue at hand. Additional principles and virtues can come from the Bible or other sources, or they may be intuitively held as self-evident (those come from natural law). It's important to get these additional principles and virtues into the discussion and connect them to the interests they support.

4. List the Alternatives

Given the conflict you've identified, what alternatives are available to you to resolve this conflict? Be sure to distinguish between alternatives that necessarily resolve the dilemma and those that could resolve it but might not.

5. Compare the Alternatives with the Principles/Virtues

This is the step where the ethical evaluation and assessment begins in earnest. The ideal at this step is to recognize an alternative that satisfies all of the competing moral principles and virtues. If that is the outcome, you've hit a home run, and you can likely sleep very well at night after resolving the dilemma in this way. If that doesn't happen, don't despair, since it's not that common for one alternative to satisfy all our competing principles/virtues.

The more customary way of resolving the dilemma is realizing that we have to make choices. Often, in order to make a clear decision, you must weight one or more principles/virtues more heavily than the others. When doing this, be sure to provide good reasons for emphasizing one principle/virtue above the rest. You should provide more of a basis for your weighting than simply your intuition. However, at this point, you may not yet have a clear decision, and some other factor is brought to bear on the issue. At the least, at this next step, you might eliminate some alternatives.

6. Assess the Consequences

Though consequences are not the determining factor, they should not be ignored. In the event that our principles/virtues have not yet yielded a clear decision, consideration of consequences may help weight the competing values that support the alternatives still on the table. Here the task is to take the viable alternatives and attempt to predict the likely (as opposed to speculative) consequences of each. In addition, you should try to estimate how beneficial are the positive consequences and how severe are the negative ones, since some consequences will be negligible and others will be more significant.

7. Make a Decision

At some point, you have to stop deliberating and make a choice. Often these decisions are not easy, nor are they painless. Be careful of trusting your "sleep-well quotient" too. You may make a good decision and still not sleep well, because these dilemmas are often very difficult and don't lend themselves to easy solutions.

APPLICATION OF MODEL TO CONFIDENTIALITY CASE

Let's return to the case that introduced this chapter: you are back in the role of manager with knowledge that your friend is being laid off, and he's asked you for a heads-up as to whether he's on the layoff list. Let's work through the decision model in order to illustrate how it is used.

1. Gather the Facts

- Your good friend John reports to you in the workplace. He is in your group, and you are his manager.
- John is a computer systems analyst.
- There are rumors floating around the company that some layoffs are coming because of a downturn in business.
- You know that these rumors are true.
- You know that your friend John is on the list of people who are going to be laid off.
- John likes his current job and is inclined to stay in it.
- John has been offered another job in his field and in roughly the same geographic area, but his current job offers better pay and a shorter commute.
- The company that has offered him this job is pressuring him for a decision before the layoffs will be announced.
- John has a family to support—a wife, three children, and a fourth child on the way.
- Your company has a strict policy of confidentiality that prevents you from disclosing who is on the layoff list.
- John has asked you for advance warning if he is going to be laid off.
- John has appealed to your friendship and reminded you that he and his wife are expecting a fourth child, to get you to tell him if he's on the layoff list.
- John has asked you directly if he's on the list.
- John is interpreting your silence in response to this question as indicating that he's not going to be laid off. That interpretation is obviously incorrect.

- John is important to a major project he's working on. If he found out he was on the list, he would leave early and jeopardize the project's schedule.
- You feel considerable guilt about maintaining confidentiality up to this point.
- John has made you feel guilty by asking you to consider how much he would lose if he made the wrong decision.
- John admits he would be in a difficult place if he turned down the job offer and ended up being laid off.

2. Determine the Ethical Issue

The parties with interests in this case are primarily John, you, and your company. John has an interest in maintaining his job status so he can fulfill his moral obligation to support his family. You, along with your company, have an interest in maintaining confidentiality about who is going to be laid off. Your company has a policy on this, and they take it very seriously because of their obligation to give their clients the best work they can and to give their shareholders the best return on investment they can (a fiduciary obligation).

The conflict is between John's interest and the interests of you and your company. John has an interest in knowing whether he is about to be laid off, and both you and your company want to keep that information confidential. The moral principle/virtue underlying John's interest is the obligation to take care of his growing family by taking a responsible approach to his job security—a burden for which you have great compassion. On the other hand, you have a moral obligation of loyalty to your company, one that is reaffirmed every time a paycheck is directly deposited into your bank account. We could summarize the conflict this way: *compassion toward your friend for his responsibility to his family versus the obligation of being loyal to your company by acting in their best interests.*

3. What Other Principles/Virtues Have a Bearing on the Case?

John is being motivated in part by self-interest in the desire to stay employed and keep regular paychecks coming. But his major motivation is his sense of obligation to take care of his family, fulfilling a biblical responsibility (2 Thess. 3:10–12; 1 Tim. 5:8). He is committed to his family's well-being, which he believes will be jeopardized if he is unemployed.

But that is also true for you, if you breach confidentiality and are fired for it. You are motivated by the virtues of compassion and friendship toward John, and you realize he is in a very difficult position. John also acknowledges that the virtue of friendship should prevent him from putting you in this tough position, and he is conflicted about that too. You rightly recognize that you have a moral obligation to give your company your best work, also a biblical responsibility (Col. 3:23–24).

4. List the Alternatives

There are two clear and obvious alternatives—to keep confidentiality and not tell John anything about the layoff list, or to breach confidentiality and tell him that he's about to be laid off. Both of those clearly solve the dilemma, though neither of them satisfies all the principles and virtues. But there are other options that you can entertain. Given that he has already asked you if he's on the list, and if he could interpret your silence as indicating that he's not going to be laid off, it is difficult to see how you could tell him indirectly. You could answer him in a generality by saying, "It's wise for anyone these days to be prepared for layoffs," thereby encouraging him to accept a sure thing instead of taking a risk by turning down the other job offer. One final alternative is to put the burden back on him by appealing to your friendship, suggesting that a friend would not put you in the compromising position in which he has put you.

5. Compare Principles/Virtues with the Alternatives

In this scenario, there's no obvious win-win alternative, one that satisfies all the relevant principles/virtues. It appears that you will have to make a choice, weighting one set of principles/virtues over another. One choice is to weight the obligation to your employer more heavily than the obligation to your friend and his family. Or you could do just the opposite. Here it seems that the obligation of friendship goes both ways, toward you (to tell John whether he is going to be laid off) and toward John (to avoid putting you in such a morally compromising position).

6. Consider the Consequences

So it seems we are left with basically two alternatives: to tell John he's on the layoff list or to maintain confidentiality. There are several ways you could do either of these options. What are the likely consequences of these alternatives?

If you decide to tell him, the *positive outcomes* include the following:

- John wisely accepts the job offer, knowing he will be laid off.
- His family remains in a good financial position.
- Your friendship is protected, and John is grateful to you for looking out for him.
- You avoid guilt for keeping the information from him.

The *negative consequences* likely include:

- Your job and your ability to provide for your family could be jeopardized if it gets out that you told John he is on the layoff list.
- John leaves the company to take this new job before his current project is finished, leaving the company shorthanded, which reflects badly on you.

Conversely, if you decide to maintain confidentiality, the likely *positive consequences* include:

- Your job remains safe because you have not violated a company policy that is strictly enforced.

- Given his skills, John will likely not have trouble finding another job in his field, even if he turns down the job he was offered.

However, if you maintain confidentiality, the likely *negative outcomes* include:

- John can't make a wise decision about this new job offer.
- If he turns down the job offer and is laid off, he will jeopardize his family, at least temporarily, and he will be angry with you.
- Your friendship will be strained because of your unwillingness to disclose this information to him. It is unlikely that the families will spend as much time together.

7. Make a Decision

This comes down to how you weight the competing principles/virtues of loyalty to your company versus compassion for a friend. On the surface, it would seem that compassion should be weighted more heavily, given the potentially difficult consequences for John should he turn down the new job offer. But the virtue of friendship turns both ways. You could make a good case that no close friend would put another friend in a position to lose his job by violating company policy. Therefore I would more heavily weight the value of loyalty to my company and the obligation to do what is in their best interest, and I would not break confidentiality. If John presses me with the question again, I would insist that I can't tell him and that I do not appreciate him putting me in this position, pointing out that a good friend would not do that.

CONCLUSION

You don't have to agree with my decision in this case; that's why they are called moral dilemmas! It may be that you see some of the elements differently, and that's okay. My hope in this chapter is that you find this to be a useful process to help you make decisions when facing genuine moral dilemmas, which, remember, involve a conflict between two or more principle/virtue-driven interests. Sometimes in a fallen world, principles/virtues—even explicitly biblical ones— can conflict, and choices have to be made. Hopefully, this procedure will help you think hard and well about those decisions.

Review Questions

1. How do you recognize an ethical dilemma when confronted by one?
2. What are the steps involved in resolving an ethical dilemma?
3. Take an ethical dilemma you are facing now, or have faced in the past, or could anticipate facing in the future, and apply the decision-making model to that situation.

For Further Reading

Rae, Scott B., and Kenman L. Wong, *Beyond Integrity: A Judeo-Christian Approach to Business Ethics,* 3rd ed. Grand Rapids: Zondervan, 2012. Chap. 1.

CHAPTER 5

ABORTION

How can you say that a pregnant seventeen-year-old, for whom having the baby will ruin her life, is doing something wrong by having an abortion?

Consider this scenario. Your next-door-neighbors have a seventeen-year-old daughter who is a star student, has been accepted to a prestigious college, and has a very bright future. She and her boyfriend, who have been together for only a few months, had a moment of passion that got away from them, and she has recently told her parents that the pregnancy test was positive. Predictably, her boyfriend wants nothing to do with the baby and has no interest in having a pregnant girlfriend. She is understandably distraught and feels like she is facing this alone. Her parents are pressuring her to "get it taken care of," meaning end the pregnancy and get on with her promising life.

Your daughter is one of her best friends, and this girl has confided in her about the pregnancy and asked her what she thinks she should do. Your daughter has now come to you for advice about what to tell her. What would you say? How should your daughter respond to her friend's questions about ending this pregnancy?

Very few moral issues are more hotly debated and, culturally, farther from resolution than abortion. And very few moral issues are so heart wrenching emotionally as facing an unwanted pregnancy, especially at such a young age, with all of your adult life ahead of you. This suggests that there is an important pastoral dimension to attend to before any discussion of the morality of ending the pregnancy. This young woman needs to know that she is loved and supported by her family and the people close to her, that her life is not over, even though it feels like it, and that there are good solutions to the dilemma she is facing. This is not to say there are easy solutions, but she needs to know that the situation she is facing is not hopeless.

ABORTION AND THE LAW

In virtually all countries in the developed world, abortion is legal, at least until viability, and in many other countries well after that. Abortion laws can be somewhat more restrictive in the developing countries, though for some time the trend has been toward legalizing abortion all over the world. In some countries, such as China, especially during its one-child government policy (now changed to a two-child allowance), the incidence of abortion is considerably higher, and in parts of the developing world, infanticide and child abandonment are more routinely practiced.

In the US, abortion is legal through all nine months of pregnancy. The combination of Supreme Court decisions handed down on the same day in January 1973 essentially legalized abortion on demand. The companion decision to the well-known *Roe v. Wade* decision, *Doe v. Bolton*, clarified the exception made in *Roe* in the third trimester that legalized abortion for a threat to the life or health of the mother. The *Doe* decision outlined what constituted the threats to the health of the mother, which included physical, emotional, and psychosocial threats and what the court called a familial threat to the mother's health. This last threat had to do with the number of children the woman was raising, most often on her own, and the court decision made an exception that allowed for abortion in the case of her having more children than she could reasonably take care of.

The *Roe* decision further made the woman's physician the one who decided what constituted a threat to her health, indicating that it was a private decision between a woman and her doctor. This is why today, third-trimester abortions are legal in the US and why there is such debate over so-called partial-birth abortions. For minors, parental consent for abortion is not required, since a girl may appeal to a "judicial bypass" of her parents if she believes that disclosing her pregnancy to them would result in harm to her.

Infanticide is illegal in the US, and physicians practice under the "Born Alive Rule," which states that any child born alive (even if it is the result of a failed abortion) has the right to life and therefore cannot be killed or abandoned. However, infanticide is still widely practiced in some parts of the world, with baby girls overwhelmingly the victims of either direct infanticide or abandonment that results in their death. Support for legalizing some forms of infanticide is growing more worldwide in the academic bioethics community, with it now being referred to as "after-birth abortion."

ARGUMENTS TO JUSTIFY ABORTION

Let's go back to our young woman in the scenario that opened the chapter. Suppose she has decided to end her pregnancy, and you have the opportunity to ask her about her rationale for the decision she has made. What do you think are the primary reasons that she believes warrant her decision? Of course, it's possible that she has simply made her choice and doesn't care about whether it is morally justified. But for many women with unwanted pregnancies, this decision is a profoundly moral one and is appreciated as such.

She might give the reason that it's my body and therefore my choice. This is the most common rationale for abortion, coming out of a deeply rooted view of personal autonomy and privacy that pervades the cultures of the West. It often functions as a "trump card" argument, effectively ending any discussion. It is true that what is called a right of bodily integrity is central to the right of privacy. For example, physicians cannot force treatments on adults against their will, assuming the person is capable of making rational decisions. In most states, if doctors force unwanted treatments onto their patients, they can be charged with battery. But if we look a bit closer at this rationale for abortion, it runs into some trouble.

Let's start with the premise of this argument, that the baby is part of the mother's body. Technically, that's not quite true. The baby is actually a separate entity with an entirely separate genetic code, and in roughly half of the pregnancies, a different sex. From very early on in the pregnancy, the baby has its own circulatory and nervous systems. It is true that the baby is dependent on the mother's body. But being dependent on the mother and being part of the mother are two different things. This rationale for abortion confuses the fetus being attached to the woman carrying it and being a part of the woman carrying it. It does not follow that just because the fetus is attached to its mother by an umbilical cord that the fetus is a part of her in a way that denies its own separate identity.

Here's something else to think about with this rationale. Only on the assumption that the fetus is not a person does this argument of "my body, my choice" make sense. That is, if the fetus is not a person, it makes sense for the mother's right over her own body to take precedence. But if the fetus is a person, it makes no sense to insist that the mother's choice should take priority over the fetus's right to life, because life always takes precedence over the exercise of freedom when they conflict. Further, only by assuming that the fetus is not a person can a woman justify ending its life simply because she chooses to do so.

Philosophers call this "begging the question," that is, assuming your conclusion at the very start. This rationale assumes that the fetus is not a person, for if it is a person, the argument doesn't work. Of course, pro-life advocates aren't allowed to beg the question either and assume the fetus is a person; that premise also requires a defense. Actually, if the fetus is a person, he or she has a claim on the mother's body for the support necessary to survive. Hopefully, the discussion of this justification for abortion focuses on the right question—whether the fetus should be recognized as a person with the right to life.

The young woman in the opening scenario might also give the reason that *no one should have to bring an unwanted child into the world*. A child could be unwanted for a variety of reasons; the idea that "having this baby will ruin my life" is the main one. It could likely create financial and lifestyle hardship for this young woman if she decides to raise the child alone. Of course, it may be that her parents will shoulder a major part of the burden. Or in the next few years, she may meet someone who will embrace both her and her child.

But let's think a bit further about that rationale for ending the pregnancy. The young woman is defending her abortion choice because the baby is unwanted for the hardship it would likely cause her and itself later on as a child. But again, only with the assumption that the fetus is not a person does this argument have any merit. For if the fetus is a person, then surely "hardship does not justify homicide," as philosopher Frank Beckwith puts it. In addition, if the fetus is a person, then the argument based on unwantedness justifies taking the lives of many adults who are widely perceived as unwanted, including the homeless and the severely mentally challenged. Unwantedness is ultimately a commentary on the mother, not the fetus. Whether a child is wanted or not has nothing to do with its moral status as a person.

Children can be unwanted for other reasons besides the hardship they might produce. What if the baby has a *genetic abnormality* that would leave the child facing a lifetime of challenges? Though this is not the case with our young woman, this reason begs the question like the others, since only with the assumption that the fetus is not a person does it make any sense. For if the fetus is a person, ending his or her life because of a genetic anomaly would justify, by extension, ending the lives of adults with similar challenges. But most cultures don't widely envision that, precisely because the persons in question are indeed persons, with full rights to life, irrespective of their ability to function.

To be sure, this respect for life at the margins is eroding, as the recent support for infanticide suggests. But before accepting this reason for abortion, consider how presumptuous it is to assume that there is a necessary connection between disability and unhappiness. The notion that disability gives someone a life not worth living, or that they would have been better off never having been born, is both false and insulting to the disability community. I suspect that if you took an informal poll of genetically challenged kids, asking them, "Do you think you would have been better off never having been born?" you'd be met with incredulous looks.

Children are also unwanted because in rare cases *they are conceived as a result of sexual assault.* It's understandable that a woman would not want to carry a child resulting from rape or incest. But to use that as a justification for abortion turns something understandable into something justifiable, and those are two quite different things. How a child is conceived is irrelevant to his or her moral status as a person. This argument too assumes that the fetus is not a person, and if that assumption is true, then abortion could be considered part of a woman's self-defense against sexual assault. But if the fetus is a person, then surely one act of violence against a person does not justify a second, against the baby.

To go back to our young woman with the unwanted pregnancy who insists that having the baby will irrevocably alter the trajectory of her life, that is not necessarily true. It is the case that the pregnancy will change at least the next nine months of her life, until the baby is delivered. But she can put the baby up for adoption if she chooses to make that difficult but heroic decision.

Here the young woman might object (as do many pro-choice advocates), saying, "You have no idea how hard it is to put a baby up for adoption." For most people who have not done this themselves, she is probably right. But let's look a bit closer at this objection and ask, what makes putting a baby up for adoption so difficult? For some, it's the shame involved, and that may be part of specific cultural traditions. But for most, they rightly recognize that adopting out a child is not like selling a car or a home or parting with cherished possessions. What makes it different is that the woman has experienced a connection and bonding to the baby.

Severing that connection, even immediately after birth, is difficult and heart wrenching. But that bonding, as real as it is, doesn't happen with things. It is true that selling a home that one has owned for some time produces grief and a sense of loss, but that is generally about the memories and relationships the house reflects, not the building itself. This kind of bonding that makes adoption so challenging happens not with things but with persons, with whom it is possible to form connections and relationships, even in the womb. The difficulty of putting a baby up for adoption supports the notion that fetuses are indeed persons and that adoption, however difficult, is a far better option than abortion. The Bible treats adoption with nobility, as it is the most common metaphor used to describe our relationship to God.

Other arguments that pro-choice advocates commonly put forward have to do with the law on abortion: first, that restricting abortion, especially legally, is discriminatory against poor women, since they don't have the resources to procure the abortion in places where it would be legal; and second, that restricting abortion legally will force women into illegal, and therefore unsafe, conditions for abortion. The argument based on discrimination is a clear case of begging the question, since calling a restriction on abortion discrimination assumes that access to abortion is something all women should have. Yet that is the very point under debate, and people who use this argument have clearly assumed their conclusion in order to make their case. The contention that women will be forced into unsafe conditions for abortions misrepresents what occurred prior to *Roe v. Wade* in 1973. In reality, most abortions before 1973 took place in licensed facilities with properly licensed physicians, though there were some exceptions to this general rule.

THE CASE FOR THE UNBORN

Assuming that the young woman in our scenario wants our advice, think about how you would explain to her that the unborn child she is carrying is a person with the right to life and the right to the protection of the mother. Beginning with biology, here are two points on which everyone agrees and which science can verify. First, the fetus is *alive* in the womb, and second, he or she is *human*. Thus the question, when does life begin? or even, when does human life begin? can be answered easily—at conception.

From conception forward, the fetus is both alive and human. If it were neither, then scientists would not be nearly so interested in harvesting its stem cells. The question worth asking is not the biological one but the philosophical one. When does human *person-hood* begin? That's the question for which science cannot provide a definitive answer, since it's fundamentally a philosophical inquiry, not a scientific one.

If the young woman is coming to this from a Christian world-view and takes the Bible seriously, this next part of the discussion may be all that is needed to establish the case for the unborn. At the least, the Bible teaches that *abortion stops the handiwork of God in the womb*. This is the clear teaching of biblical texts such as Psalm 139, which describes the prenatal skill and care of God in fashioning the unborn child. Psalm 139:13–16 puts it this way:

> You created my inmost being;
>> you knit me together in my mother's womb.
> I praise you because I am fearfully and wonderfully made;
>> your works are wonderful,
>> I know that full well.
> My frame was not hidden from you
>> when I was made in the secret place,
>> when I was woven together in the depths of the earth.

> Your eyes saw my unformed body;
>> all the days ordained for me were written in your book
>> before one of them came to be.

This psalm does not explicitly make the case that the unborn child is a full person, but there is a clear continuity of personal identity throughout the stages of the psalmist's life, from the earliest points of pregnancy, when he was an "unformed body," to adulthood, as he's described in the first part of the psalm. In other words, the psalmist David is the same person both in the womb and as an adult, and is treated as such by God. This parallels the way several places in the OT equate the child in the womb and the adult (Jer. 1:5; Job 3:3). In fact, the Hebrew term for a baby is also used to refer to a young child and even a young adult.

In the NT, from the earliest points of pregnancy in the life of Jesus, it is clear that the Bible is describing a full, image-of-God-bearing person. In Luke 1–2, the celebration of the coming of the Messiah begins not with his birth but with his conception. To be sure, there is also a great celebration at his birth. But when Mary, uniquely knowing from the moment of conception that she is pregnant, visits her relative Elizabeth, who at the time is pregnant with John the Baptist, the celebration of the Messiah's coming begins— roughly five to seven days after Mary has conceived. Mary and Elizabeth believed that the Messiah had come with his conception.

Even if someone is skeptical toward the Bible's teaching about the personhood of the unborn, it is clear that in the womb, God is working to accomplish something very special. He is weaving and forming the child with great skill and care. It's as though a pregnant woman has a sign on her abdomen that says, "God at work—do not interrupt!" Abortion not only terminates the life of the child; just as important, it stops the creative handiwork of God. For someone who takes the biblical teaching as authoritative, this should be sufficient to make the case for another option besides abortion to deal with an unwanted pregnancy.

It is true that abortion is also killing an innocent person, but making the case for that may not be necessary at this point in the discussion. Of course, if the young woman in our scenario has no regard for the Bible or is not a follower of Jesus, then little of the biblical teaching will be relevant, and another line of reasoning is required.

If the young woman insists that at this stage of the pregnancy, the fetus can't possibly be a person, that raises this question for her to consider: *if the fetus is not a person at conception, then at what point does it become one?* The burden is then on her to make a case for another point between conception and birth at which there now exists a person with the right to life. This is under the assumption of the law that at birth the fetus is a full person, though advocates of infanticide would dispute that.

Consider the other junctures, often known as "decisive moments," at which it would be possible to think that a full person now exists. Why not follow the law and insist that at *birth* there now exists a full person? The problem with taking birth as a decisive moment is that birth is primarily a change of location, and a slight change in the degree of dependence on the mother. Neither location nor dependence have any necessary connection to the moral or ontological (referring to one's essential being) status of the fetus.

This is the reason for the increased support for infanticide, now called "after-birth abortion." Advocates of this view rightly recognize that there is nothing ontologically special about birth. Unfortunately, they have drawn the conclusion—opposite to the law's determination—that because the newborn and the fetus are not ontologically different, neither have the right to life. The pro-life supporter concludes that because birth makes no difference, both the unborn and the newborn are full persons with the full right to life.

The notion that location has no bearing on the moral status of the fetus also holds for another commonly suggested decisive moment, though this one doesn't apply to our scenario, since the young woman is already pregnant. Some people hold that *implantation* is the phase of pregnancy at which you have a full person. That is, embryos outside the womb are not persons, but once implanted, they are, especially given that the womb is the only place suitable for embryos to develop in. But implantation, like birth, is merely a change of location and is thus irrelevant to the fetus's moral standing.

Neither is it germane that the fetus cannot develop outside the womb for very long. The suitability of a location is not ontologically relevant. If I forced you to live on the moon, a place currently unsuitable for human beings, you would not be any less of a person, even though you wouldn't thrive in that environment. Your potential for flourishing does not determine your moral status, though your moral status does suggest the obligation for anyone responsible for your well-being to provide an environment in which you can flourish.

The young woman in our scenario might also make the case for viability as the moment that matters for the determination of personhood. Viability refers to the ability of the fetus to survive outside the womb. This occurs at roughly twenty-three to twenty-six weeks of pregnancy, though it can vary from fetus to fetus. Viability actually varies more widely, depending on access to specialized medical technology. These early-in-the-pregnancy viability dates assume that this technology is available in a neonatal intensive care unit (NICU). This is why viability was considerably later in pregnancy decades ago, before the advent of today's NICU medicine. So viability is variable and not a fixed point that is the same for every pregnancy. As a result, viability measures the *state of medical technology*, not the moral status of the fetus. This disqualifies it from being an adequate decisive moment, since it has no necessary connection to the fetus's ontological standing.

Our young woman might suggest that the onset of *brain activity* is the best decisive moment, though at her current stage of pregnancy, about forty-five days into it, the fetus inside her is close to having brain waves. This decisive moment makes sense to the young woman because of the parallel with the definition of death, which is indicated by no brain activity. Since the end of brain activity is what determines death, or the loss of personhood, she holds that it is reasonable to take the beginning of brain activity as the indication of personhood.

However, a fetus without brain activity for the first four to five weeks of pregnancy is significantly different from the dead person who is permanently without brain activity. The brain of the developing fetus is only *temporarily* nonfunctional. Also, the embryo, from the point of conception, has all the necessary capacities to develop full brain activity. Until about forty-five days of gestation, those capacities are not yet realized but are latent. Just because a capacity is not exercised is not a necessary comment on the essence of the fetus, since that capacity is only temporarily latent, not irreversibly lost.

A final decisive moment the young woman considers is called *sentience*. This refers to the ability to experience sensations, namely, but not limited to, pain. She suggests that if the fetus cannot feel pain, then the harm in abortion is minimized, and that to be a person, someone must be able to take an interest in his or her interests. However, this decisive moment confuses the experience of harm with the reality of harm. It does not follow that the fetus cannot be harmed simply because the fetus cannot feel pain or otherwise experience harm. Even if I am paralyzed from the waist down and cannot feel pain in my legs, I am still harmed if someone amputates my leg. Having interests and being able to experience those interests are two quite different things. Even people who cannot experience a setback in their interests can nonetheless have their interests genuinely impeded. Even the deceased can have their interests thwarted if their wishes are ignored or their will is disregarded.

From this discussion of the various decisive moments that could be used to determine when a fetus becomes a person, we could make a case that goes something like this: since we all can agree that all human persons are the result of a process of development that begins at conception, and since there is no break in the process that has moral or ontological significance for the status of the fetus, then it follows that we have a person from conception forward. Because of this, and to insure that our language matches our view, the embryo does not *develop into* or *become* a fetus. Rather embryos *mature into* fetuses, which mature into newborns, toddlers, adolescents, and adults. A human being doesn't gain or lose personhood moving from one stage to the next. He or she simply matures.

After realizing that there is no valid moment between conception and birth where she can logically assign personhood to the fetus, our young woman might suggest that what matters is not the point along the continuum but the ability of the fetus to perform certain minimal functions common to all human persons. These include consciousness, self-awareness, the ability to interact with one's environment, a capacity for relationships, and some ability to reason. This list can vary somewhat but normally includes the above functions. Once the fetus, or the baby after birth, can perform these required functions, they would be designated persons, with rights and protection.

Many advocates of this way of viewing persons would admit that it opens the door to infanticide within the first few weeks or months after birth. They further admit that since persons possess these qualities in a more-or-less fashion, then personhood becomes what philosophers call a "degreed property." That is, being a person is not an all-or-nothing proposition but is a matter of degree. People who are at the beginning of life—that is, fetuses and newborns—are less of a person, and the same would be true of people at the end of life, when those capacities diminish. In addition, people with severe disabilities that affect those critical functions would be less of a person, if at all.

The primary limitation of viewing persons this way is that it doesn't account for situations in which someone has temporarily lost those functions, such as when under general anesthesia or in a reversible coma. Anyone under general anesthesia, assuming it works as designed, cannot perform any of those critical functions.

Yet no one considers their personhood compromised or lost, since it is only a temporary situation. But that is precisely the case for the fetus in the womb. Those functions are temporarily latent, but from conception forward a fetus has the capacity to perform all those functions. Those capacities have yet to become evident, but they will as long as the maturing process is not interrupted.

A final argument the young woman might make is to concede that the fetus is a person but insist that her right over her own body trumps the fetus's right to life. She might cite the example of the world-renowned violinist who needs a nine-month blood transfusion in order to live. Since you're a perfect match to her blood type, you are drugged and kidnapped. When you awaken, you find yourself hooked up to the violinist and are told that if you unhook yourself, the violinist will die. You then conclude that surely you are not obligated to stay connected to the transfusion machinery for nine months and that the violinist's situation is tragic but irrelevant to yours. The young woman believes this is analogous to an unwanted pregnancy, that even if the fetus is a person, the mother is not obligated to render nine months' worth of aid, even if failing to do so results in the fetus's death.

Though this analogy appears to fit the unwanted pregnancy situation nicely, there are some major differences. First, since you were kidnapped and forcibly connected to the transfusion apparatus, this is more analogous to a pregnancy that results from nonconsensual sex, not a pregnancy in which sex is freely engaged in. Also, pregnancy is not comparable to imprisonment, though rarely some pregnancies require full bed rest and other significant limits on activity. Further, the violinist is a complete stranger. Surely, this is not the same as one's child (remember, the young woman has already conceded that the fetus is a person).

Once the woman has admitted that the fetus is a person, the better analogy is that of a newborn. Imagine that you and your spouse have a newborn child, age four months. The baby has not been sleeping for more than a couple of hours at any one time, and both of you are exhausted and desperately need a break. So you decide to take a two-week vacation, just the two of you. But instead of making arrangements for the baby, you prepare enough bottles of formula for two weeks, and you stack two weeks' worth of diapers in the nursery. You then kiss your baby goodbye and leave.

Upon your return, who do you think would be there to "greet" you? Angry neighbors, incensed relatives, Child Protective Services, and the police—all of those, and possibly others, would be very interested to see you on your return. The police would likely arrest you and charge you with child endangerment, and, given the high likelihood that your baby died while you were gone, you would also be charged with negligent homicide with callous indifference, if not murder.

On what basis would you face those charges? What exactly did you do wrong? You violated the fundamental rights of the baby—not only the right to life but also the right to receive what he or she needs from the parents to survive and flourish. We would say that if this is a right of the baby, then *the baby has a claim on the parents* for the resources he or she needs to live and thrive, subject to the ability of the parents to provide them. Of course, if the parents cannot provide at least the minimum of these resources, the state will place the baby into an arrangement where those means are available.

If this is true for a newborn, why is it not also true for the fetus? Remember, the young woman has already admitted that the fetus is a person with the right to life. Once she has conceded this, then the mother's right over her own body doesn't trump the baby's right to life. *The baby actually has a claim on the mother's body* for the resources necessary to live and thrive. That's a claim you don't often hear about, but one that follows from the concession that the fetus is a person, a sentiment that is growing, given the ability of technology to look more clearly at the maturing baby in the womb.

ON EMBRYOS, STEM CELLS, AND FETAL TISSUE

It's one thing to consider unborn children in the womb as being persons with the right to life, but it's quite another to think the same of embryos outside the womb, who are invisible without a microscope. It strikes many people as odd to think of embryos prior to implantation as the moral equivalent of unborn children in the womb and newborns outside the womb. Viewing embryos as a source of stem cells, potentially useful for suffering patients, further complicates the moral issues. In addition, the video evidence that abortion providers such as Planned Parenthood routinely and callously engaged in the black market sale of tissue from aborted fetuses raises the moral issue of the use of this tissue from elective abortions.

If, as we have argued so far, a person with the right to life exists from conception forward, then harvesting embryonic stem cells (normally done at the three-to-five-day stage of development) is the moral equivalent of aborting fetuses or killing newborns in order to harvest their organs and tissues. To be clear, human embryos are not the only source of stem cells useful for medical treatments. In fact, they are not even the primary source of stem cells for treatments currently in use.

It's important to distinguish between types of stem cells. In general, *pluripotent* stem cells are the undifferentiated cells that in theory can be programmed to become any of the cell types in the body. They are the "blank slates" of stem cells. Pluripotent stem cells come from embryos, mainly those left over from infertility treatments. But there are also *multipotent* stem cells that are not quite blank slates but have some differentiation that limits the types of cells into which they can be engineered. For example, neural stem cells can in theory be programmed to become any neurological type of tissue, but since they are already a bit down the developmental pathway, they cannot become blood cells. Similarly, stem cells harvested from umbilical cord blood won't help someone who has a brain or spinal cord injury.

The great majority of stem cell treatments in use at present are using stem cells derived from *nonembryonic sources*. Pluripotent stem cells hold considerable promise, but development of treatments using embryonic stem cells has lagged far behind, in part because of issues of compatibility with the patient. Just as a bone marrow transplant must have a donor who is an exact match for the recipient, stem cell treatments require precise compatibility (in fact, a bone marrow transplant is a type of stem cell treatment), and stem cells from leftover embryos are rarely a match for the recipient. Most nonembryonic stem cells (often called "adult stem cells") are harvested from the patient who will receive treatment, insuring a match. Adult stem cells are not in any way morally controversial.

What's at issue is the pluripotent stem cells harvested from human embryos, a process that at present results in the death of the embryo. A promising type of pluripotent stem cells are called *induced pluripotent stem cells* (iPS), which come from a process in which cells from the adult body of the patient are "reprogrammed" and coaxed to go backward on their developmental pathway, enabling them to become embryo-like entities that have pluripotent stem cells, which are similar to stem cells harvested from human embryos. This is an example of a technology that may resolve an ethical dilemma instead of creating one.

When it comes to the moral status of embryos outside the womb, remember what we said earlier about the notion of implantation being the decisive moment for personhood. We said that implantation marks a change in location only and that location is irrelevant to a person's moral and ontological status. We also said that a location's unsuitability for the embryo is also irrelevant, since if I sent you to the moon, you couldn't flourish, but that would not matter to your designation as a person. Location does not determine moral status. Neither does size. Embryos are not simply clumps of cells; from the first stage as a single-celled fertilized egg, the embryo has all the capacities it will ever have—however latent—and is a finely structured organism.

Philosophically, our common views of a person assume a *continuity of personal identity*. For example, we assume that human beings continue to be the same person irrespective of time and change. Our social notions of moral responsibility and criminal justice are dependent on this view of personal identity. Metaphysically, this is called a "substance" view of a person. Another way to say this is that being a person is a matter of one's *essence*, or nature, not the ability to perform certain functions. Only an essential view of a person avoids the problematic idea that being a person is a matter of degree.

Once it is admitted that being a person is a matter of essence, then the continuity of personal identity follows. Once we admit to a continuity of identity, then there is no place along the continuum from conception to birth where there is a valid decisive moment. The result is that one is a person from conception forward. The single-cell embryo has all the genetic information it needs to mature into a full-grown adult, needing only shelter and nutrients. If implantation does not make a morally relevant difference, then whether embryos are implanted in the womb or stored in the lab is irrelevant to their moral and ontological status.

A slightly different argument applies to the sale of tissue from aborted fetuses, for which Planned Parenthood and other abortion providers have come under intense criticism. Not only has the use of fetal tissue become commercialized, but also both the timing and manner of the abortion procedure have been affected in order to maximize the harvest of it. For example, the later in the pregnancy that the abortion occurs, the more mature the tissue that is harvested. In addition, since many abortion methods do violence to the body of the fetus, methods of abortion that tend to leave more of the fetal body intact, such as a C-section, are preferred. Initial proponents of obtaining tissue from elective abortions (as opposed to obtaining it from spontaneous miscarriages, which is the parallel to organ donations from adult donors) insisted that it not be bought and sold on the open market, or black market, and that neither the timing nor the method of abortion be altered. These practices are not uncommon today, as the video evidence against Planned Parenthood indicates.

But even if it's not bought and sold and the abortion procedure is not changed, there are still moral issues with using the tissue from elective abortion. Given how it was obtained, it is not hard to argue that the tissue is morally tainted. It would be similar to having a well-organized system to procure the organs of two-year-olds by the parents authorizing the death of their child. Most people would argue that the benefits of using those organs are irrelevant compared with the immoral means by which they are obtained. It's only with the assumption that the fetus is not a person that one can make any argument in favor of using this tissue. In addition, the mother who authorizes the abortion is hardly in a position to consent to the donation of the tissue. In fact, the system confuses the donor with the donation. The deceased fetus is the donor, not the mother.

Some people have suggested that the use of this tissue is comparable to using the data from the Nazi experiments performed during WWII on concentration camp inmates. They argue that the data can be separated morally from the experiments themselves in a way analogous to separating the fetal tissue from the abortion procedure. The difference is that the Nazi experiments are, thankfully, no longer occurring today. But that's not true of the abortion procedures. If the Nazi experiments were still going on today, there would be little debate about using the information gleaned from them. The focus would be on stopping the heinous experiments. Similarly, for people who hold that abortion is a violation of the unborn child's right to life, the tissue obtained in this way is morally tainted. It was a good thing that the practice of Planned Parenthood in this commercial market for fetal tissue was exposed when it was.

CONCLUSION

The debate over abortion and the moral status of fetuses and embryos has proven to be particularly resistant to resolution over the past decades and does not look to be resolved in the near future. Technology is making it more difficult to hold that the unborn is a "product of conception" or "piece of tissue," and the consensus is changing, though slowly. Some pro-choice advocates are conceding that the fetus is a person yet are arguing that the mother has the right to end the life of her full-person, unborn child. More people are recognizing that the abortion decision is a grave moral decision, regardless of one's view of the moral status of the unborn child. This debate is likely to continue for the foreseeable future, and there will be continued need to protect the most vulnerable among us, particularly the unborn.

Review Questions

1. What advice would you give to someone with an unwanted pregnancy who is considering abortion?
2. How would you defend the idea that the unborn child is a person from conception?
3. What are the different "decisive moments" often used to determine when a fetus becomes a person?
4. How would you defend the idea that embryos are persons?

For Further Reading

Beckwith, Francis J. *Defending Life: A Moral and Legal Case against Abortion Choice.* New York: Cambridge Univ. Press, 2007.

George, Robert P., and Christopher Tollefson. *Embryo: A Defense of Human Life.* New York: Doubleday, 2008.

Kaczor, Christopher. *The Ethics of Abortion: Women's Rights, Human Life and the Question of Justice,* 2nd ed. New York: Routledge, 2014.

Lee, Patrick. *Abortion and Unborn Human Life.* Washington, D.C.: Catholic Univ. of America Press, 1996.

CHAPTER 6

REPRODUCTIVE TECHNOLOGIES

What do you say to infertile couples about the hi-tech ways to have a baby?

Consider the following scenario. You are sitting across the table from a couple who have been wrestling with infertility for the past three years. There is no apparent medical reason for their lack of success in achieving a pregnancy. They have been very open with you about their struggle in this area and how much pain it has caused them. They tell you that their individual senses of gender identity have been challenged by their inability to conceive a child.

They tell you about the well-meaning friends who tried to encourage them but ended up being more hurtful than helpful. They have grown isolated from their friends, all of whom seem to be having no trouble becoming pregnant. They have even stopped going to baby showers, because these are painful reminders of their failure to conceive.

The couple have recently been to the local infertility clinic and came back with several options that are both high-tech and high-priced. Some of the alternatives involve donors contributing genetic material, and in some cases a surrogate who would carry and give birth to the baby for them. They are puzzled by the array of options to consider and have come to you for counsel. They specifically want to know which, if any, technological options are consistent with the Bible. They have some friends who told them that since the Bible commands us to be fruitful and multiply, any technological option is acceptable. They also have some friends who believe it's wrong to use anything but natural means to get pregnant, which would rule out all the technological options and relegate them to adoption. They are open to adoption but consider it a last resort if all else fails.

TECHNOLOGICAL OPTIONS FOR INFERTILITY

On their visit to the infertility clinic, they were presented with an array of ways in which medical technology can assist a couple to achieve a pregnancy. Some are relatively inexpensive and not necessarily high-technology. Others are quite the opposite. The specific medical reason for infertility generally determines which technologies are indicated. Methods on the lower-technology end of the spectrum include intrauterine insemination (IUI), with the sperm of the husband or that of a known third-party donor. IUI simply involves a little extra push, which doesn't quite occur naturally, to help sperm get to the egg.

If there is no clear reason why the couple cannot become pregnant, IUI is usually the first option. Donor insemination (DI) normally utilizes the sperm of an anonymous donor, who is paid a small fee for his donation. Some sperm donors donate multiple times, as films such as *Delivery Man* and *The Kids Are All Right* indicate. Use of donor sperm is common among single women and lesbian couples who want to have a child.

Egg donation is used frequently when the infertile woman is older (late thirties to forties) or if she is unable to release eggs. In reality, women rarely donate their eggs. They sell them, and calling the process a donation is not quite accurate. The process of harvesting eggs is much more involved than that of harvesting sperm. The donor undergoes what is called "ovarian hyperstimulation," in which strong hormones are used to enable the woman to release as many eggs as possible in one thirty-day cycle. The norm is roughly ten to fifteen eggs, but some women have released as many as fifty to sixty in one cycle. The eggs are surgically removed from the uterus and must be fertilized in the lab shortly after harvesting.

When an infertile couple buys eggs from a third party, they are normally fertilized with the husband's sperm, outside the womb, and the resulting embryos are then implanted in the womb of his wife, or that of a surrogate who will carry the pregnancy in her place. Surrogacy is sometimes necessary if the woman is unable to carry a child to term. A woman is normally paid from $2,500 to $5,000 per harvest of eggs. Higher prices are sometimes offered if the woman selling the eggs meets specific physical criteria such as height, eye and hair color, and intelligence.

By describing egg selling, we are well on our way to understanding the most common high-tech method for conceiving children, *in vitro fertilization* (IVF). IVF involves harvesting eggs from the infertile woman, then fertilizing them in vitro (Latin for "in glass"), normally with the husband's sperm. The embryos created by successful fertilization are then implanted in the woman's uterus, and if all goes well, she becomes pregnant and gives birth to a child, or to multiple children. This is because the norm is for one to four embryos to be implanted at any one time, to increase the chances of a successful pregnancy, which gives the couple the possibility of twins or triplets. Any embryos that were created but not implanted are frozen and stored for use later if the couple does not become pregnant.

Normally with IVF, if the procedure results in a multiple pregnancy in which there are more children than the woman can safely carry, or if the couple simply don't want as many children as she is pregnant with, the clinic will refer them to another facility that will selectively terminate some of the implanted embryos. If the couple becomes pregnant with the number of children they want and have embryos left over in storage, they must make decisions about the disposition of the remaining embryos.

Other technologies that are not used as frequently as IVF include *GIFT* (gamete intrafallopian transfer), which is almost the same as IVF except that fertilization occurs in the body instead of in the lab, and *sperm injection*, in which a single sperm is injected into the egg, all done in the lab. Sometimes a combination of egg harvesting and IUI is used, in which the woman releases multiple eggs, but instead of being harvested, they remain in her womb and IUI is performed, normally with the husband's sperm. This combination can create complications involving a multiple pregnancy. Normally, infertility physicians won't use these technologies together unless the woman agrees in advance to reduce the number of embryos should she become pregnant with major multiples (four or more children).

Other technological options involve surrogates, who agree to carry a child to term for another woman or infertile couple. The most common form of surrogacy is called *gestational surrogacy*, in which the surrogate has no genetic connection to the child she is carrying. This type of surrogacy requires IVF, and the embryos created in the lab are then implanted in the surrogate, who carries the child and gives birth. Immediately thereafter, she normally turns over custody of the child to the couple who has contracted her. In many states, this type of surrogate has no rights to the child she carries, so if she changes her mind and wants to keep the child, she is required by law to turn the child over to the contracting couple.

Gestational surrogates are most often paid a sizeable fee (tens of thousands of dollars) in addition to all medical expenses. Increasingly, surrogacy is outsourced to women in developing countries, who are willing to serve as surrogates for a fraction of the fee charged in developed countries. Surrogates (and egg donors) are an increasingly common option among gay male couples desiring to have a child.

Rarely used today, because of potential legal complications, but used frequently in the early days of surrogacy is what is known as *genetic surrogacy*, sometimes referred to as *traditional surrogacy*. This occurs when the surrogate is genetically related to the child she is carrying, having had IUI with the sperm of the contracting couple. The legal obstacles occur when the surrogate changes her mind and wants to keep the child. Since it is her egg and her womb, she is considered the legal mother of the child and cannot be forced to relinquish her child unless she is unfit as a mother. Thus custody would be shared with the genetic father.

It is not hard to see why the risks involved with this would deter most couples from this option, even though it is medically less invasive and cheaper financially. This is because genetic surrogacy involves only IUI and not IVF. Genetic surrogacy was ruled by some courts to be baby selling and has been outlawed in many states. Gestational surrogacy is generally considered "prenatal babysitting," and the fee paid to the surrogate is for womb rental, not the purchase of the child, though some states in the US and some countries around the world prohibit both types of surrogacy.

THEOLOGICAL CONSIDERATIONS ON TECHNOLOGICALLY ASSISTED REPRODUCTION

One of the primary questions that our infertile couple want your help with has to do with what the Bible teaches on reproductive technology. That is, what limits, if any, does the Bible place on the couple in the use of medical technology to become pregnant? Of course, they are also interested in other factors, such as the cost and success rate of various technologies. But they are committed to being faithful to Scripture in this important area of their life together.

In general, there are three moral positions that are most commonly adopted. The most restrictive is that of official Roman Catholic teaching, which insists that most technological options are not morally acceptable. This teaching distinguishes between technologies that *assist* normal sexual relations and those that *replace* natural sex. Those that replace sex in marriage are deemed morally unacceptable, since, in this view, they violate God's intention and design for sexual relations.

On the other end of the continuum is the view that God mandated that human beings be fruitful and multiply and gave humanity medical technology as a gift of common grace to help alleviate the effects of the general entrance of sin into the world (of which infertility is one). Proponents of this view argue that all reproductive technology is morally acceptable as long as it brings a wanted child into the world. This is also the position widely held in many cultures in the developed world, based on the freedom of couples to exercise their right to try to have a child.

A position more in the middle, between these two, is taken by many Protestants, who hold to some modest restrictions on the use of reproductive technology, based on several important biblical and theological principles.

Since the biblical authors do not directly address any of the specific technological options our couple are facing (though in biblical times, surrogacy was considered the most common way to alleviate infertility and was widely used), this raises the question of exactly how the Bible speaks to this issue. There are no "chapter and verse" passages in the Bible that clearly spell out what is morally acceptable and what is not, so what the Bible gives our couple is broader and more general principles that form the boundaries around the use of these technologies. Perhaps the best way to illustrate this is by calling these theological considerations "fence posts" that give the couple the parameters, within which there is freedom. But should they go beyond the fence posts, they run into a theological danger zone, where they are outside the biblical boundaries.

Our first fence post involves *the place of medical technology*. In the Genesis account of creation, God gave human beings the task of exercising dominion over the world, making human beings his trustees over the created order, to use it responsibly for their benefit while protecting the resources at the same time. The task of dominion became more complicated after the entrance of sin into the world and involved alleviating the effects of sin as much as possible. As the Wisdom Literature makes clear, God also embedded his wisdom in the world (Prov. 8), and through his common grace (grace made available to all human beings regardless of their faith commitment) and general revelation (God's revelation to all human beings) gave human beings the ability to discern this wisdom.

One of the results of this common grace is the development of various technologies to make life better and especially to counteract the general effects of sin in the world. Medical technology is one of the primary good gifts of God to all human beings to enable us to lessen the burden of disease, death, and decay that came as a result of sin. Since infertility is clearly the result of the entrance of sin into the world, and not part of God's original design, it would appear that the use of some medical technology to deal with infertility would be acceptable.

The official Catholic objection to the use of technology for infertility is their belief that God's design for sexual relations in marriage requires that the unitive and procreative aspects of sex always go together. That is, the one-flesh aspect of sex (the unitive) must always be accompanied by openness to procreation. Thus a couple cannot separate sex and procreation, by means of artificial birth control or abortion; nor can they engage in procreation apart from sex, by means of technologies that replace normal sex, such as IUI and IVF (assisting sex is considered proper). Any third-party participation in the process is also considered morally unacceptable, ruling out sperm and egg donors and surrogates.

Although Protestants may share some things in common, such as skepticism about third-party contributors, most have more modest restrictions on the use of technology in this area. It is not clear that the Bible requires that the unitive and procreative aspects of sex always be joined. Song of Songs praises the joy and pleasure of sex, with no mention of a procreative purpose. Similarly, when the NT counsels single adults and praises marriage as the appropriate context for sexual expression, it does so by highlighting the pleasure and unitive aspect of sex, again with no mention of the procreative aspect. It seems that the Bible treats the unitive aspect as in itself a sufficient end for sex, and separating the unitive and procreative aspects can be acceptable. In fact, menopause seems to be a natural and God-ordained separation of the unitive and procreative aspects of sex; after menopause, it's hard to see how a couple can be meaningfully open to procreation.

So it would seem that some technological options are available to our infertile couple seeking to achieve a pregnancy. But that does not mean that all of them are morally acceptable. Though it is true that God gave an original mandate to be fruitful and multiply, the goal was to fill the earth, and one could easily argue that this task has been fulfilled, many times over. The mandate to procreate, by itself, does not mean that all technological options are acceptable. Medical technology, particularly to alleviate infertility, is also subject to the reality of sin and therefore is a qualified good, meaning that it can be beneficial but can also have morally problematic aspects. Most technologies are mixed in this way, with positive elements and things to be concerned about.

A second fence post about which the Bible is clear is the *sanctity of life from conception*. Since this notion was addressed in the previous chapter, we won't revisit that discussion here. The Bible's view on the personhood of an unborn child means that couples utilizing technology to achieve pregnancy cannot be involved in any option that compromises the sanctity of the child's life. For example, most physicians will not perform IUI in conjunction with the ovarian hyperstimulation hormones that enable multiple egg release, unless the couple agrees to have the number of resulting embryos reduced if necessary. This type of selective abortion also occurs in IVF if more embryos successfully implant than the woman can safely carry. These are very problematic situations, but the couple can prevent them by avoiding the combination of IUI and multiple ovulation or by not agreeing to have more IVF embryos implanted than the woman is able to bear.

Somewhat more complex is the common scenario with IVF, in which a couple has embryos left over in storage after the process is complete. This often happens when the couple achieves a successful pregnancy or a multiple pregnancy. The couple then faces a difficult decision on the disposition of these embryos, which are not clumps of cells but their children. A commitment to the sanctity of life from conception precludes discarding these embryos, which is the normal practice in many IVF clinics. Donating the embryos to research or to harvest their stem cells, both of which will result in their destruction, is the moral equivalent of discarding them. Couples often put off this decision by simply storing the embryos indefinitely, which is not a solution, since at some point the embryos cannot be thawed successfully, making it too the equivalent of discarding them.

The moral principle that governs IVF in this regard is that all embryos created in the lab are owed an opportunity to mature in the womb. The best solution is for the couple themselves to carry them to term, thereby assuring the continuity between procreation and parenting. But if that is not possible (in some cases for medical reasons), it would be acceptable for the couple to put their embryonic children up for adoption. They would donate their embryos to another infertile couple through "embryo adoption." Some adoption agencies facilitate these arrangements, such as the Snowflake Program in California.

One way to minimize the number of embryos created at the beginning of the process is to reduce the number of eggs harvested, by limiting the ovarian hyperstimulation hormones. Or the couple can ask for the GIFT (gamete intrafallopian transfer) procedure, even though it is not widely used today because it is more invasive. In this procedure, the eggs are harvested as in IVF, but only some are placed back in the woman's body, in the fallopian tubes with sperm so that fertilization can occur in the body as opposed to in the lab. Normally, a maximum of four eggs are used in GIFT, and the rest are fertilized in vitro. The couple can request that the remainder of the eggs be discarded and not fertilized at all, leaving them with a single attempt at pregnancy through GIFT. This can be an expensive way to utilize this technology, since if it fails, the couple has no recourse except to start over from the beginning, as opposed to simply thawing out embryos in storage. But it would guarantee that the couple would have no leftover embryos at the end of the process.

A third fence post comes out of the above mention of embryo adoption. The Bible holds *adoption* in high regard, a part of the overall biblical teaching on the obligation to care for the vulnerable. Orphans needing adoption are a very common figure of speech in the Bible, representing the most vulnerable among us (James 1:27). In addition, adoption is the most common metaphor for the believer's relationship to God, since the believer has been adopted into God's family by virtue of Christ. The high place the Bible puts on adoption does not mean that a couple should not pursue technological options. But it does call into question an infertile couple who insist that they wouldn't consider adoption or who would consider it a last resort only.

A fourth fence post comes out of the Genesis account of creation and is not always easy to apply. Genesis 1–2 upholds *the sanctity of marriage as the context for procreation.* In the Genesis narrative, the normative context for procreation is permanent, monogamous, heterosexual marriage. If you take the two complementary accounts of creation in Genesis 1–2 (Genesis 1 gives the panoramic overview, and Genesis 2 the more specific account of the creation of human beings and their relationship to God) and put them in chronological order, God creates male and female, institutes marriage, and then gives the mandate to be fruitful and multiply. This all suggests that marriage precedes procreation and forms the normative context for procreation. There is an ordained continuity between marriage, procreation, and parenting. That is, people who procreate are intended to take responsibility for their procreative actions.

What makes this parameter more complicated is that there are several unusual ways of procreating children in the OT that seem to depart from this context but are not necessarily considered sin. For example, surrogacy was widely practiced in the ancient world and was the only remedy for infertility. Abraham and Sarah had a surrogate, Hagar, which ended badly because of Abraham and Sarah's lack of faith in God's promise to bring them a natural heir (Gen. 16). It ended so badly that the biblical author did not see any need to comment further on it. But Jacob also had surrogates (Gen. 30), without the catastrophic conclusion that Abraham, Sarah, and Hagar had. Similarly, levirate marriage (Deut. 25:5–6) occurred when a woman was widowed childless. Under the law, the nearest next of kin was obligated to marry her and raise up a child to carry on the lineage of her deceased husband, making this practice somewhat analogous to sperm donation. However, it was required for the next of kin to *marry* her, reinforcing the normative context of marriage for procreation, even in this unusual set of circumstances.

Other examples that seem to be at variance with the creation mandate for family include polygamy, allowed in the OT but prohibited in the NT, and divorce, allowed under certain conditions because of humankind's hardness of heart (Deut. 24:1–5; Matt. 19:8–9). In terms of interpreting the Bible, nothing necessarily follows from these allowances about the norm for procreation today. Just because they occurred in OT times does not mean they are necessarily allowed today.

It seems that the rest of the biblical writers took the norm of creation quite seriously. For example, when the prophets accused Israel of idolatry, the most common figure of speech they used was adultery, in referring to idolatry as "spiritual adultery." Their appeal to the norm of marital faithfulness as the basis for condemning idolatry comes out of the creation account, which set faithful monogamy as the norm. If that were not the case, the parallel between adultery and idolatry would make little sense.

Further, when the NT authors refer back to the creation account, they consider it a very strong argument to make their case. Take, for example, Paul's allusion to creation when addressing homosexuality (Rom. 1), or the place of women in the church (1 Tim. 2), or Jesus's teaching on divorce (Matt. 19). In each of these examples, the biblical author gives the Genesis account great weight and offers no other argument to make the case compelling; the appeal to the creation account was considered sufficient.

What this suggests is that the creation account should be taken as a norm for marriage and procreation, meaning that procreation should occur only within the confines of marriage. This would make the introduction of third parties into the matrix of marriage (sperm or egg donor, surrogates) prima facie problematic from the perspective of the biblical norm for procreation. This would also suggest that single adults should refrain from procreation, though they can and should be encouraged to adopt, either born children or embryos. This recognizes that adoption introduces third and fourth parties into the process, thus on the surface making adoption seem problematic.

But *adoption is not procreation*. Adoption is a heroic rescue, something fundamentally different from procreation. No one should be precluded from heroic rescues, unless they are unfit to parent. For couples that need a sperm or egg donor, embryo adoption can be a good alternative. This gives the couple much of what is important to them in procreation, namely pregnancy and childbirth, though it does not give them the genetic connection they may deeply desire.

CONCLUSION

To summarize, in view of the biblical parameters for procreation, technologies that utilize the genetic materials of husband and wife are generally within the biblical boundaries. These include IUI, IVF, and GIFT as well as a sperm-injection technology in which a single sperm is injected into a single egg in the lab. With IUI and IVF, the couple must insure that they avoid the selective termination of fetuses in the womb and the discarding of embryos in storage. Technologies that involve egg, sperm, or womb donors are generally problematic, involving a third party entering the matrix of marriage for purposes of reproduction. They further undercut the intended continuity between procreation and parenting, which should give both men and women pause before considering donating sperm or selling eggs.

Women who are seeking to sell their eggs have an additional

concern about the safety of the process. It is not uncommon to have what has come to be known as "ovarian hyperstimulation syndrome," which involves a variety of potential complications, including loss of future fertility. The infertility industry maintains that egg harvesting for donation or sale is a safe procedure, but there is no data to support that claim. The reason is that the "donors" are not tracked after they complete the process of "donation." The clinics that harvest their eggs do not follow up with them unless they have immediate complications that require the clinics to provide follow-up care or referral to hospitals. We simply don't know about the long-term risks of this process, because there is no data available.

Concern is also evident in surrogacy, since a successful surrogacy arrangement requires the surrogate to distance herself emotionally from the child she is carrying, something we'd never otherwise encourage a woman to do. There is considerable debate over the question of motherhood in surrogacy arrangements, though the law has settled this by essentially denying all rights of parenthood to gestational surrogates, putting them in the position of being human incubators. There is additional concern about the way in which surrogacy is being outsourced today to developing countries, at a fraction of the cost compared with prices in the US or in the countries in Europe in which it is legal. Many of the women sought out as surrogates are desperately poor, increasing the potential that they will be exploited.

Infertility technology is a wonderful gift of God when used within the boundaries prescribed by Scripture. The pain of infertility is real and deep, and medical technology can be a good solution if practiced within the parameters of biblical teaching. Adoption remains as a heroic rescue highly valued by the Bible, and increasingly couples are choosing adoption as a first resort, not a last.

Review Questions

1. How would you answer the question posed at the beginning of this chapter: what would you say to an infertile couple about the hi-tech ways to conceive a child?
2. List some of the ways in which technology can assist procreation today.
3. What do you think the Bible teaches about using technology to assist procreation? What principles are important to consider?
4. Which technological options for infertile couples do you think fit within the biblical and theological parameters discussed in this chapter?

For Further Reading

Best, Megan. *Fearfully and Wonderfully Made: Ethics and the Beginning of Life.* Downers Grove, Ill.: InterVarsity Press, 2012.

Rae, Scott B., and D. Joy Riley. *Outside the Womb: Moral Guidance for Assisted Reproduction.* Chicago: Northfield, 2011.

CHAPTER 7

GENETICS AND BIOTECHNOLOGY

What do you tell couples who want to use biotechnology to produce "designer children"?

Since the Human Genome Project was completed in the early 2000s, an explosion of genetic information has been available to individuals who want to test for various genetic links and risks. As a result, medicine has learned a great deal about the genetic component to a wide variety of diseases and conditions.

Many new genetic tests are available, both for unborn children in the womb and for adults with a family history of disease. These tests can reveal not only direct genetic links, which will cause disease, but also genetic predispositions, which do not necessarily cause a particular disease but increase the risks of developing it. Biotechnology is also available to select the sex of one's child and, less reliably, to select some specific traits, marking the first time in history in which prospective parents can seriously consider producing "designer children." In addition, some biotechnology normally used to treat specific conditions can now be used to enhance otherwise normal traits.

The ethics involved in these various technologies are quite complicated, especially since the consensus in the culture is, "If we can do it, we ought to do it." Some advocates, knows as "transhumanists," have the goal of using biotechnology to transcend humanity, producing human beings who are free from the normal limitations of being human. The danger of this view is that it might undermine what it means to be a human being made in God's image, and produce a "brave new world" that, in the end, we discover we don't want.

GENETIC TESTING

Imagine you and your spouse have just found out that you are pregnant. As the pregnancy progresses, you will be asked if you want to undergo several different genetic tests for your child in the womb. These range from simple blood tests to ultrasound imaging, which can rule out many genetic abnormalities, to sophisticated tests such as amniocentesis and chorionic villi sampling (CVS), both of which allow the baby's cells to be tested directly. In most cases, if these simpler tests indicate a cause for concern, the more advanced tests then occur. For women over the age of thirty-five, amniocentesis and CVS are routinely offered because of the increased risks of birth defects.

If the couple receives bad news on these genetic tests, they are considered candidates for genetic counseling, after which they have to make a difficult decision about whether to keep the pregnancy. It is common for couples to end the pregnancy in these cases, and it is widely reported among couples facing this decision that they have experienced varying degrees of pressure from their physician to end the pregnancy. At the least, couples often feel as though they have to justify their decision to keep the pregnancy. Couples should be aware that even though the margin of error is small on the more advanced tests, the degree of challenge is difficult to predict. For example, Down's syndrome exists on a continuum from moderate challenge to severe deformity, and a couple won't know where their child is on that continuum until he or she is born.

If we reflect on our previous discussion of abortion and the personhood of the unborn from conception forward, this raises difficult ethical issues when it comes to ending the pregnancy in these cases where there is a genetic abnormality. The child with a genetic defect is no less a person than a child who does not have genetic problems. In fact, the argument that abortion is justified in cases of genetic anomaly assumes that the unborn child is not a person. Otherwise, the argument would support eliminating newborns, toddlers, and adults with similar genetic conditions, which we clearly don't consider, precisely because they are persons deserving of dignity and respect.

Frequently, the decision to end the pregnancy in these cases is made based on a highly debatable premise. It is not uncommon for couples to justify the abortion on the grounds that they are helping their child avoid a "life not worth living." However, couples should be very careful not to assume that there is a connection between disability and unhappiness. That assumption is presumptuous and is considered insulting by the disability community.

This is not to underestimate the challenges of living with, and caring for, a child with genetic problems. But if we took a poll of children with genetic challenges and asked them if they thought they would be better off having never been born, I suspect they would consider that a very odd question. I suspect they are glad to have been born and think of their lives as valuable and worth living. Further, it would not be unusual for the parents to have the same thoughts and feelings toward their child, that they could not imagine their lives without their child, and consider their lives richer for their child being part of them. This is the case even with very severe challenges, such as those in which children are born terminally ill and imminently dying, as in the case of anencephaly, in which the child is born with only a brain stem. These children live just a few weeks on average, but parents routinely report that they are glad they have had the chance to hold their child, if only for a short time.

Couples who have a history of genetic issues and want to avoid passing along those risks altogether consider what is called "preimplantation genetic diagnosis" (PGD). Following conception through IVF, the embryos have cells removed, analogous to a biopsy (the procedure is sometimes known as "embryo biopsy"), and the cells are screened for the specific genetic abnormality for which the child is at risk. The embryos that are free of the suspected anomaly are then implanted in the womb, and the ones that have the genetic problem are discarded. Though this seems, on the surface, to be a responsible way to avoid genetic risks, remember that embryos are persons too. Discarding embryos is the moral equivalent of aborting fetuses. There is little moral difference between discarding genetically defective embryos as a result of PGD and aborting genetically defective fetuses as a result of amniocentesis.

This raises a quandary for couples who have a risk of genetic disease. Take this couple, for example. The man is thirty-two, and the woman is twenty-nine. She has the genetic link for Huntington's disease, a terrible, degenerative neurological disease in which the person suffers progressive neurological deterioration. Symptoms don't usually onset until the midthirties to midforties, though in some cases much later. The person lives an entirely normal life until then, though they are living with what they feel is a ticking genetic time bomb. This couple was opposed to abortion and to discarding embryos, so the usual methods of preventing genetic disease for their child were justifiably not considered options for them. Their choices were to attempt pregnancy naturally, with a 50 percent risk of passing on the Huntington's gene to their child, or to accept childlessness. At that time, because of the mother's likelihood of developing the symptoms of Huntington's disease, they were not considered candidates for adoption.

How would you advise them in this difficult dilemma? What would you do if you were facing this decision? Though many people would understandably choose not to subject their child to these risks, it is probably too strong to insist that there is an obligation not to procreate naturally in this situation. After all, the child is still an image-of-God-bearing person with dignity and value, regardless of his or her genetic condition, and will have a very normal life for many years.

Sometimes a person with a genetic history does not know for sure if he or she has the genetic condition that will cause the disease. They face a decision that is prior to the decision to procreate naturally. They face the decision to be tested themselves. Consider another couple, roughly the same ages as the pair we've already met. The man's father has Huntington's in his family but has never been tested for the gene himself. He is in his mid-sixties and has yet to develop symptoms, and his sense is that the genetic defect has bypassed him. His son and his wife, who are about to start trying to have a family, are pretty sure they have nothing to be concerned about. If the Huntington's gene has bypassed the man's father, then it has certainly bypassed him too, and they can start a family without anxiety.

But they recently received a phone call from his father informing them that he has begun to experience Huntington's symptoms, and though he has not been tested, he is sure he is in the beginning stages of Huntington's disease. Now the son is wondering if he has the genetic defect that will give him Huntington's, and their decision to start a family has become much more complicated. He has to decide whether to be tested at all, a more difficult decision than it would appear, since the majority of people with Huntington's history choose not to be tested. His wife will support either decision, but she is eager to know if they can procreate naturally. She does not want to be past childbearing years only to find out that he is free of the problematic gene and they could have procreated naturally. The ability to test adults as well as children for genetic conditions raises dilemmas like these. I encouraged him to be tested, out of concern for his wife's desire to have children naturally but avoid the risk of passing on the Huntington's gene.

Though most couples use genetic testing to avoid genetic risks, in some cases they use biotechnology in order to intentionally produce a child with a genetic abnormality. Imagine a couple who are both deaf, who desire to have a nonhearing child. They could employ a variety of technological options to achieve that end. They reason that they could not adequately parent a hearing child. Further, they insist that deafness is not a disability, and that nonhearing persons have a richer experience of the other senses as a result of their deafness. However, it seems problematic to preclude important options for the child, such as hearing, since it would be counter to a well-accepted moral principle of a child's right to an open future.

This principle suggests that one important way that parents seek the best interests of their children is by keeping the child's future open so he or she can make as many of life's important choices as possible. Of course, parents are right to preclude some options for their children that are obviously harmful to them. Theologically, one can make a good argument that God designed human beings to be hearing and that to deliberately produce a child without that capacity is a violation of God's design and intention.

SEX SELECTION

Biotechnology can be used today to reliably select the sex of a couple's child, what many people consider the first step toward designer children. Of course, the option of sex selection is not new, but the ways in which it was practiced involved destruction of the child who was not the desired sex, through either abortion, infanticide, or discarding embryos of the nondesired sex. However, through a sperm-sorting technology known as MicroSort, a couple can select for sex without being involved in any of the above practices, since the selection is done prior to conception. Sperm obtained from the husband is separated by whether it has the X or Y chromosome. The sperm that produces the desired sex is then used in IUI in order to achieve fertilization and a successful pregnancy.

One reason why couples might want to do this is to avoid a sex-linked genetic abnormality, of which there are roughly three hundred. Conditions such as muscular dystrophy and types of hemophilia are sex-linked in this way. But most couples who use MicroSort technology do so for another reason—family balancing.

Of course, if a family uses this technology because they believe one sex is inferior to another, that is highly problematic. But most couples who desire family balancing have no intrinsic preference for one sex over another. They want both because they value both so highly.

Consider a couple with two boys and a desire for a third child, with a longing for that child to be a girl. They have stated that they want a third child only if they could have reasonable assurances that it would be a girl. But they have made it clear that they will love and accept a third child regardless of the sex, even though they strongly prefer to have a girl at this stage of their lives. They are asking you what you think of the option of using MicroSort to increase their chances of having a girl. They also are strongly desirous of remaining faithful to what the Bible teaches but are unclear about what exactly it does teach on this subject. What would you tell them about the option of MicroSort?

It is not uncommon to have an intuitive response to this that suggests that the couple is "playing God" in using technology to select the sex of their child. But it's not always clear how that phrase is being defined, and as a result, it can become a vague objection to practices that strike us as problematic although we can't quite articulate why.

Sometimes the phrase is used to argue that a person or couple should not engage in actions that could undermine the sovereignty of God. But there is an important difference between undermining God's sovereignty and undermining trust in God's sovereignty. Human actions, particularly through the use of technology, are not capable of undermining God's sovereignty, though using technology can certainly undercut a person's trust in God's providence. That is, MicroSort does not, and cannot, undermine God's sovereignty, though it is quite capable of undermining a couple's trust in his providence. To be clear, the phrase "playing God" refers to actions that usurp prerogatives that belong to God alone. The debate here is whether determining the sex of one's child is one of those things to which God alone is entitled.

It seems clear that choosing the sex of the child is a valid use of medical technology if the goal is to avoid sex-linked genetic disease, since genetic abnormalities are the result of the entrance of sin into the world. But its use more generally, for family balancing, is more complicated. I would question the use of the phrase "family balancing" to describe the desires of the parents here. The use of this phrase suggests that there is something unbalanced about the current makeup of this family.

From a Christian worldview, that would seem to be suggesting that there is something defective about the family that God has sovereignly given to these parents. But surely that's not the case if we hold that God, in his providence, has given this family these particular children. In addition, if the goals of medical technology, from a Christian worldview, are to alleviate, relieve, and contest the diseases and medical conditions that are the result of the general entrance of sin, then MicroSort would be acceptable only on the grounds that the sex of the child is a result of the fall. But gender is not a disease, regardless of how it might be viewed in some parts of the world. This suggests that technology for sex selection might be outside the theologically legitimate goals of medicine and that couples should accept their child's sex as one of the givens of life, to be received with gratitude.

The Bible is clear that children are a gift from God (Ps. 127:1–3). Since gifts are normally given without strings attached or expectations except gratitude, this suggests that children are to be received gratefully, openhandedly, and without specifications. It would seem that to put specifications on a gift could undermine the nature of the gift as freely given and gratefully received. To be sure, there are some exceptions to this, such as wedding registries and children's Christmas lists, and the reason why we allow for this is that our knowledge of our loved ones is imperfect, though if the specifications become too numerous or precise, we raise valid questions about their appropriateness. But God's knowledge of us is complete and perfect, meaning that he doesn't need information from us about our desires in order to bestow perfect gifts upon us.

A further question for this couple concerns the expectations they have for the sex of the child they so desire. It may be that the couple not only wants a girl but also wants a certain type of girl, which she may or may not grow up to be, and this could serve to reinforce harmful or limiting gender stereotypes on the child. It may be that the child does not live up to the gender expectations of the parents or feels pressure to become someone she is not. Part of the joy and responsibility of parenting is to allow the child as much of an open future as possible, helping to bring out the person whom God has uniquely made, rather than seeking to make the child in the parents' images.

GENE EDITING AND DESIGNER CHILDREN

Through a recently developed technology, gene editing is now being done. The process, known as Crispr-Cas9, is a new procedure that enables scientists to snip out defective genes and replace them with the corrected version, thus treating genetic disease right at the source. A protein called Cas9 functions as a genetic scalpel, and repair enzymes enable researchers to seal the resulting gap with new genetic information, thus changing the underlying genetic code.[1] This has exciting promise to deal with a variety of genetic abnormalities far more efficiently than does traditional gene therapy, which has failed to live up to its initial promise since its inception more than thirty years ago.

In an extension of this technology, Chinese researchers performed a similar kind of gene editing on human embryos.[2] The embryos were nonviable, and the process had a fairly low success rate, producing what are called "off target" mutations, in which the

---

1. Jonathan Rockoff, "Why Gene-Editing Technology Has Scientists Excited," *Wall Street Journal* (June 28, 2015), *www.wsj.com/article_email/why-gene-editing-tech nology-has-scientists-excited-1434985998-lMyQjAxMTA1MTE5NDUxMzQ5Wj*.

2. David Cyranoski and Sarah Rearden, "Chinese Scientists Genetically Modify Human Embryos," *Nature* (April 22, 2015), *www.nature.com/news/chinese-scientists -genetically-modify-human-embryos-1.17378*.

procedure affected other parts of the genome in ways scientists hadn't anticipated. This raised concerns about the procedure's safety in embryos, particularly since the genetic changes, both intended and unintended, would be inheritable by successive generations, making it a form of what has long been called "germ line therapy." But it raises for the first time the ability of science to do the kind of gene splicing and replacement necessary for producing designer children.

Though the researchers insist they have no intention of using the technology for genetically altering traits, the technology to perform gene splicing and editing, though still in its infancy and not yet ready for public consumption, is here, waiting for someone to use it to do genetic alterations for non-disease traits, thereby producing designer children. Designing children is being done today in more crude ways, such as selecting the traits of gamete donors (unreliable), using PGD to screen for particular traits (costly), or using abortion or infanticide (mostly for sex selection).

BIOTECHNOLOGY AND HUMAN ENHANCEMENT

Many different medical technologies and biotechnologies have dual uses—to treat disease and clear medical and psychiatric conditions and to enhance otherwise normal traits. For example, human growth hormone (HGH), originally used as a treatment for dwarfism, is now routinely used for children who are at the lower end of the normal range for height. In addition, beta-blockers, which have a variety of uses, namely to treat social anxiety disorders, are now being used by professions for whom steady hands and calm nerves are critical to performing their jobs, such as concert musicians and even surgeons. Further, Ritalin, the drug that treats ADHD, is often sold on the black market on college campuses for students who have no diagnosable ADHD but are looking for heightened concentration and focus (known as "executive function") around final exam times.

Other biotechnologies slow the effects of aging (on muscles and memory), flatten out the emotional lows of life's difficulties (PTSD medications), treat depression and anxiety without psychotherapy, and enhance mental acuity where there is no diagnosable illness (known as "steroids for the mind").

To be sure, many forms of mental illness have a brain chemistry component that has gone askew, and the medication works miracles in giving people back their mental health. But the concerns raised about these enhancement technologies are about medicalizing notions such as sin and as a result minimizing the moral component, as medicine and biotechnology become more prominent and as genetics is used to explain more and more behavioral issues.

Further concerns are raised about accepting the limits of our humanity, as opposed to the work of the transhumanists in attempting to overcome our human nature. What do we accept as life's givens, and which of our limits can and should be altered or improved? Those are difficult questions, made more complicated by the fact that most people work very hard to overcome their limits and enhance their traits, using many methods no one questions, such as exercise, music lessons, and Kaplan courses. Why should people not enlist the services of medicine and pharmacology to assist them in this? One reason to consider is the analogy with steroids, that using them cheapens legitimate achievement, even when they are used as a supplement to hard work. On the other hand, most people would likely have no objection if their neurosurgeon took a beta-blocker to make his or her hand a bit steadier when operating on their brain.

A further difficulty in this area is making a careful distinction between treatment and enhancement, a topic that has long troubled bioethicists. Even when setting this distinction within a theological framework—in which affecting those conditions that are the result of the general entrance of sin into the world is considered treatment, and affecting those that are not the result of sin is considered enhancement—there is still ambiguity about where lines can be drawn. For example, there are some conditions for which treatment is considered acceptable, yet it's difficult to insist that they are the result of sin in the world. Take male pattern baldness, for example. It's not the norm, but it's hardly clear that it's the result of the fall, yet we have no problem with treating it as best we can. Or take orthodontics, as another example. The times that it fixes TMJ problems aside, most orthodontic work is for cosmetic purposes, yet I don't hear many people insisting that crooked teeth are the result of the entrance of sin.

What this suggests is that though it might be clearer at the extremes, drawing lines consistently is very challenging and will continue to be in the years to come. Since many of these procedures are expensive, some in the bioethics community are rightly concerned that enhancement medicine and pharmacology will worsen the already existing disparities between the medical haves and have-nots.

HUMAN CLONING

Ever since Dolly the sheep was successfully cloned in the late 1990s, there has been discussion about the morality of applying that technology to human beings. Most developed countries placed a moratorium on experiments in human cloning within a few years following Dolly, many of which are still in effect today. With the ability to harvest stem cells from human embryos, the discussion of cloning came back to the forefront, as the term *therapeutic cloning* was coined to describe the creation of someone's identical twin in the lab for the purpose of harvesting its stem cells at the three-to-five-day stage of embryonic development.

The more pressing societal debate is over what is known as *procreative cloning*, the procedure in which an identical twin is produced in the lab and implanted in a surrogate's womb, with the intention of creating someone's identical twin. This is what most people are referring to when they speak of human cloning. To be clear, cloning produces a copy of the genetic code, and thus it is not quite accurate to say that a person is being cloned, since identical twins are two distinct persons, often noticeably different in a variety of ways.

There are two primary areas of moral assessment when it comes to procreative cloning—the process per se and the reasons why someone would want to engage in cloning themselves or someone else. Critics of human cloning insist that cloning violates the cloned individual's intrinsic human dignity by making him or her a copy of someone else. Yet if the process is essentially doing in the lab what happens in the body when identical twins are naturally produced, we would not hold that a naturally produced identical twin has his or her dignity compromised. When it comes to the reasons why someone would want to do this, that's a different matter. Other than curiosity to see whether it can be done, or narcissism (the desire to be "immortal"), the most common reasons why people would want to clone themselves or their child are either unlikely to have much demand or clearly unethical. The unethical ones include cloning someone for whom genetics gives obvious advantages, such as super-models, and selling them on the open market.

But even proponents of cloning insist that an open market for embryos would cheapen human beings by making them objects for barter in the marketplace. Reasons unlikely to have many sub-scribers include replacing a child who prematurely died (cloning the child would make it harder for the parents to grieve and move on) or obtaining a form of health insurance in case tissue or organs were needed (assuming that the transplants wouldn't kill the cloned person), thereby rendering the cloned person merely a source of bio-logical spare parts. There are very few morally acceptable reasons why someone would want to engage in this practice. This suggests that the market, perhaps more so than morality, may actually be what will keep cloning from widespread use.

CONCLUSION

This area of genetics and biotechnology is likely the one that in the future will continue to pose the most complicated ethical issues, not only for individuals and families but also for society as a whole.

Science and technology in this area traditionally move well ahead of moral reflection, though there are encouraging signs that the ethical and legal aspects of the genetics revolution of the past few decades may be catching up. These technological issues will continue to impact individuals and families in new and unexpected ways, and hopefully the impact will be positive, informed by the appropriate limits of ethics and the law.

Review Questions

1. How would you counsel a couple who have just found out that their unborn child has a genetic abnormality and are considering ending the pregnancy?
2. How would you advise a couple who want to use sex-selection technology to balance their family?
3. What does the Bible indicate about the process of producing designer children?
4. What do you think of the ethics of human procreative cloning?

For Further Reading

Mitchell, C. Ben, et al. *Biotechnology and the Human Good.* Washington, D.C.: Georgetown Univ. Press, 2006.

Sandel, Michael. *The Case against Perfection: Ethics in the Age of Genetic Engineering.* Cambridge, Mass.: Belknap Press, 2007.

CHAPTER 8

DEATH, DYING, AND ASSISTED SUICIDE

Don't people have a fundamental right to die?

Brittany Maynard was a beautiful twenty-nine-year-old woman who was diagnosed with a terminal brain tumor, with a prognosis that included pain and uncontrollable seizures. At the time of her diagnosis, she lived in California, where physician-assisted suicide (PAS) was not legally allowed. So she decided to move to Oregon, the first US state to legalize PAS, and after establishing residency there, she took her own life with the assistance of her physician. Her celebrated case was a significant part of the impetus to get a PAS bill through the California legislature and signed into law in late 2015.

Imagine that your father has been recently diagnosed with a terminal illness and given roughly six months to live. He has seen some of his closest friends die in hospitals with tubes, tests, and treatments all the way until they died. It seems to him that some of the treatments, expensive and invasive, were only delaying an inevitable death. He is fearful that should he lose the ability to make decisions for himself about his treatments, his family will not be able to let him go. He is a Christian, and he is pretty sure he doesn't want his homecoming with the Lord to be delayed in the way he has seen it happen with his friends. He wants to put his wishes in writing, in what is called an *advanced directive*, or *living will*, to insure that his family members follow his desires for his end-of-life care. He doesn't want to have CPR and wishes for a DNR (do not resuscitate) order.

He doesn't want to be on a ventilator should he lose the ability to breathe, or feeding tubes should he lose the ability to take food and liquids by mouth. He doesn't want any aggressive treatments, fearing the loss of his quality of life, but only wants to be kept comfortable, in a regimen of what is called *palliative care*, which is pain relief only. If the pain cannot be adequately controlled, he wants the assistance of his physician to commit suicide.

Your father has asked you to be the one to make decisions for him, if and when he loses the capacity to make decisions for himself. Your job would be to enforce the terms of the advance directive when it comes time to make those decisions. You wonder how making those decisions fits with your convictions about the sanctity of life. You have an uneasy feeling that if you turned off a ventilator and your father died shortly thereafter, somehow you would have contributed to killing your father. You especially wonder about not providing feeding tubes if he cannot eat or drink by mouth. That seems almost inhumane to you, that you are in some way starving or dehydrating your father to death. You further wonder if your father's desire to forego aggressive treatments indicates a lack of his faith in a miracle-working God.

As you consider what your father has asked of you, you wonder about which of his wishes for his end-of-life care you could fulfill in good conscience, especially that final one about enlisting the assistance of a physician to enable him to take his own life.

The ethical issues at the end of life include both the withholding or the withdrawing of treatments, particularly life-sustaining treatments such as ventilator support and feeding tubes, and PAS or euthanasia. To be clear, termination of life support (TLS), PAS, and euthanasia are all different things. Terminating treatments, especially life support, at one time erroneously called "passive euthanasia" (incorrect because it is neither passive nor euthanasia), refers to stopping treatments so the underlying disease or condition can take its natural course, which is the actual cause of death for the patient. PAS occurs when the patient enlists the services of a physician to take his or her own life, normally through ingesting medication that will cause death. Euthanasia takes place when the patient is too ill to take his or her own life, and the physician administers the life-ending medication personally, making the intentional action of the physician the actual cause of death. Removing treatments under the right conditions is fully legal throughout most of the world, PAS is legal in five US states and some of Europe, and euthanasia is legal in some parts of Europe but not in the US.

APPROACHING THE END OF LIFE

I recently spoke on this subject at my church and asked the audience of about fifteen hundred people whether they had ever walked through the end of life with a loved one. Roughly 80 percent of the people there raised their hands, indicating that they had. I then asked how many of them had been involved in decisions about life support, and approximately 50 percent of the people raised their hands. The final question was how many of them felt well prepared for the journey through the end of life with their loved one. The number of raised hands dropped dramatically, to a small fraction of the audience. Hardly anyone in that audience felt adequately prepared for what they experienced and for the decisions they were asked to make.

I recognized that both in the culture and in the church, discussions about the end of life are not common, and as a result, many family members are put into decision-making positions in which they have little if any information about the wishes of their loved one. In addition, often family members and the communities that support them don't know what they or their seriously ill loved ones need and want at the end of life.

In the aftermath of the landmark SUPPORT study in the mid-1990s, which was a wake-up call to the medical and bioethics communities concerning the less-than-optimal experience of dying in the hospital, several health care organizations set out to study further the needs and desires of patients and their caregivers so that the end-of-life experience would improve. One of these studies, known as the *Supportive Care of the Dying Project*, was conducted by a consortium of Catholic hospitals in the US. They interviewed hundreds of patients, their family caregivers, bereaved survivors, and the health care professionals who care for these patients. They asked them what they wanted and needed from the health care system at the end of life. What was so interesting about the results was, the things they wanted and needed were not primarily medical. The things they identified as important were principally personal, relational, and spiritual.

These patients and their families who cared for them and who survived their passing indicated that *they wanted to know the truth* about their diagnosis and prognosis, communicated to them often and in a timely way. They did not want the news to be sugarcoated or otherwise downplayed, and even those in cultures that tend to keep bad news from patients to avoid burdening them further wanted the truth. One of the reasons why knowing the truth is so important is that both patients and families need time *to take care of unfinished relational business.* That is, they want to be forewarned that the end might be near so that family members and close friends can say things to the patient that they need to say before he or she dies, and so that the patient can do the same.

This desire would seem to conflict with a family's common sense of denial that the end of life is near and with their desire to hang on to their loved one as long as possible. But patients and families both recognized that if they miss the chance to "close the loop" relationally with the people close to them, they will have missed out on something very important. Patients especially were insistent that *their advanced directives be followed* and not subject to reinterpretation by their families or ignored by their physicians. Most patients with advance directives had thought out their wishes and expected them to be taken seriously.

Physicians and nurses agreed that there was a *general lack of education on care of the dying* in medical education, and that physicians were not well trained for caring for patients whom they could no longer cure. They further agreed *that the pace and pressures of medical practice* often did not allow for the time necessary to care for the dying, and that end-of-life care was often relegated to chaplains, hospice, or palliative care teams in the hospital. Physicians indicated that they often felt inadequate for end-of-life discussions with patients and families and found themselves sometimes distancing themselves from dying patients and their families.

THEOLOGY OF DEATH AND DYING

How should a Christian worldview shape our view and experience of death and dying? In my fifteen-plus years as a hospital ethics consultant, I have often wanted to ask believing families (but didn't) if they really believed what they said they believe about resurrection and eternity, because it sure didn't look like they did, based on how tenaciously they were holding on to earthly life for their loved one (who may not have wanted to have his or her homecoming delayed!).

The Bible is clear that human beings are not to take innocent life (Ex. 20:13; Deut. 5:17), because human life is God's sacred gift, indicated by the fact that human beings are made in the image of God. The reason why human life is not to be taken is that God is the one who controls the timing and manner of our death (Heb. 9:27; Eccl. 3:1–2). Further, the Bible is clear that the community has an obligation to protect the most vulnerable among us, and surely the elderly and the terminally ill constitute part of that vulnerable group. The Bible further indicates that death and dying were not part of God's original design for human beings, but that death came into the world as a result of the general entrance of sin (Rom. 5:12; 1 Cor. 15:21–22).

However, the Bible is also clear that death and dying are a normal part of everyone's life on this side of eternity (Eccl. 2:14–16;

3:19–21). The reason for this is not because death and dying are morally neutral but because of the pervasiveness and universality of sin. Thus death and dying are both enemies *and* a normal, natural part of life in this world.

Yet, that is not the end of the biblical story. First Corinthians 15:50–58 indicates that death is a *conquered* enemy, which suggests that it need not always be resisted, that under the right conditions (when treatment is futile or more burdensome than beneficial), it is acceptable to say "enough" to medicine and not delay one's homecoming any longer.

I vividly remember wheeling my father-in-law out of the hospital for the last time following surgery for bladder cancer. He could speak only in a whisper, and he motioned for me to lean down so he could say in my ear, *"Don't ever bring me here again."* What he meant was, "I'm done with doctors, hospitals, treatments, tubes, and technologies that I don't want and that are making my life miserable." Though he could not articulate it this way, I think he meant to say, "I will accept the rest of my days, however many, as gifts from the hand of God, but without medicine intervening." To be clear, he was not saying, "I want to die." He was indicating a strong desire to be through with medicine.

Stopping treatments, even life support, is not necessarily equivalent to "playing God." We clarified the meaning of that phrase when we defined it as usurping prerogatives that belong to God alone, which in this case would be the direct taking of innocent life, either by suicide or euthanasia. If withholding or withdrawing treatments were the moral equivalent of killing someone—which they are not, since the cause of death is the underlying disease—then the charge of playing God might be more accurate. For the patient's family, stopping treatments may *feel* like killing a loved one, especially if he or she dies shortly after the life support if removed.

But morally, killing and allowing to die are two different actions, with two very different intentions. Most people who want treatments removed resemble my father-in-law, in that they don't want to die. They simply want to live out the rest of their days without the further intrusions of medicine. It is quite possible theologically to envision turning off life support or stopping treatments as entrusting the patient back to God. By keeping a dying patient on life support, it's possible that the family is unnecessarily delaying the patient's homecoming.

Saying "enough" to medicine is not necessarily violating the sanctity of life, since earthly life, theologically, is a *penultimate* good, not our highest good. Thus belief in the sanctity of life does not require us to keep all people alive at all times and at all costs. Neither is it a lack of faith in a miracle-working God to turn off life support. I have often wanted to say to families who expressed this sentiment (but I didn't), that if we're waiting for a miracle, then let's go for broke and turn off everything! Of course, they are waiting for a medically assisted miracle, without realizing that God doesn't need, and has never needed, medicine to work miracles. This is where our theology makes a tangible difference, as God is about to work a major miracle, healing the patient of all his or her diseases, but most likely on the other side of eternity. The paradigm of resurrection and eternity should govern the way we approach the end of life.

Of course, not every decision to stop treatment or turn off life support is morally justified, but only under specific conditions. Under the law, if a competent patient (competent means that he or she is capable of making decisions) instructs physicians to stop treatments or otherwise refuses them, the physician is obligated to stop, lest he or she be charged with battery. This is the case with an oral request or an instruction communicated through an advance directive. Most competent adult patients want to stop treatments if one of the following conditions is met: if the treatment is futile (meaning that it won't reverse an irreversible, imminent, downward spiral toward death) or, more commonly, if the treatment is more burdensome than beneficial to the patient.

If there is a reasonable hope that the patient will improve

to a quality of life acceptable to the patient, then of course the treatments should continue. If physicians are not sure about the benefit, then the default position should be to continue treatment, perhaps with an agreed-upon trial period. But it is not irrational for patients to consider that "shorter and better," in terms of longevity and quality of life, respectively, is preferable to "longer and worse." Thus even if some treatments can benefit the patient, if the burden outweighs the benefit, the patient is justified in saying "enough" to medicine.

PHYSICIAN-ASSISTED SUICIDE (PAS) AND EUTHANASIA

With the well-publicized suicide of Brittany Maynard and the 2015 legalization of physician-assisted suicide in California, PAS is back in the public discussion. Though some of the earlier and more public proponents of PAS, such as Dr. Jack Kervorkian and Derek Humphry, founder of the Hemlock Society, are no longer prominent, many organizations advocate for legalizing PAS, such as Compassion and Choices, and Dignity in Dying.

Increasingly in Europe, where both euthanasia and PAS are legal in some countries, advocates of PAS are connecting PAS with the demographic changes sweeping the developed countries, resulting in an unprecedented percentage of the population over the age of sixty-five, with a shrinking younger segment of the population available to generate the resources to support the aging population. For example, British baroness Mary Warnock, a very influential person in bioethics in Europe and a well-known advocate for PAS, has insisted that the elderly should exercise their duty to die if they have become a burden to others or to the state. She declares, "If you are demented, you are wasting the resources of the National Health Service."[1]

---

1. Kevin Yuill, *Assisted Suicide: The Liberal, Humanist Case against Legalization* (London: Palgrave Macmillan, 2013), xi.

In the US, this sentiment has been echoed by *New York Times* columnist David Brooks, who was drawing attention to state and local budget conditions following the financial crisis in 2008–10. He said, "The fiscal crisis is about many things, but one of them is our inability to face death—our willingness to spend our nation into bankruptcy to extend life for a few more sickly months."[2] British social commentator Brendan O'Neill, in the forward to Kevin Yuill's book *Assisted Suicide: The Liberal, Humanist Case against Legalization*, points out,

> Time and again, thinkers and activists who claim only to support the exercise of individual autonomy at the end of life talk openly about the fact that letting people die will save society money and resources. Indeed, this has become one of the key implicit arguments for assisted suicide, since in Melanie Reid's words, it is 'ridiculous' that a society in crisis, a society filled with more old, demented people than have ever existed before, has failed to legalize the ending of sick people's lives [by PAS or euthanasia].[3]

When someone hears the term *eugenics*, one can easily recollect the Nazi euthanasia/eugenics program of the 1930s and '40s. But the eugenic impulse did not originate there. It began in the salons of Europe and with the elites in the US, prior to the Nazis coming to power. To be clear, the Nazi program never had a beneficent purpose. It was always for eugenics, to create a master race rid of those the Nazis deemed deficient. It did slide down a slippery slope, but started at the bottom of the slope and slid further. It is not a good example of the slide from beneficent to strictly eugenic purposes. But there were some points in common in the way we think about human beings—namely, the notion that some people were "useless eaters," a phrase being resurrected today, and the dichotomy

---

2. Ibid.
3. Ibid.

between a human being and a person, both of which are causes for alarm today in the way that the elderly are being viewed.

The most common reasons for favoring the legalization of PAS are appeals to *mercy* and *autonomy*. The argument based on mercy is that if someone is dying in pain, shouldn't medicine be able to put that person out of his or her suffering? After all, the argument goes, humane people do this regularly with animals that are suffering. Why not also with human beings? Though this argument is a very effective thirty-second commercial for PAS, hospice physicians and palliative care specialists will affirm that medicine is capable of controlling virtually everyone's pain at the end of life today without the use of PAS or euthanasia. Further, most patients who request PAS don't want to die; they want their pain under control, and when their pain is controlled, their desire for PAS generally diminishes. This is why the argument based on mercy is not the primary one used in the debate today.

The appeal to autonomy, including a fundamental right to die, is the most common approach to defending PAS today. Proponents insist that the right to privacy protects the ability to make life's most important decisions—such as the timing and manner of one's death—according to a person's deepest held values, without restriction or intervention from the state. They argue that this extension of the right to privacy establishes a basic right to die that is at odds with laws prohibiting PAS. They further maintain that there is no real difference between killing and allowing to die, and that if it is legal to allow someone to die, why is it not also legal to assist them in taking their own life, under the same conditions?

Opponents of PAS respond that if there is a fundamental right to die (which the US Supreme Court denied in its 1997 decision on PAS), then it cannot be restricted to people with terminal illnesses, who have only a set period of time left to live. If it's a fundamental right, *then it's available to everyone, regardless of the reasons*. It's inconsistent to have such a substantial restriction on a fundamental right, suggesting that it's not a fundamental right at all. Further, there is a morally relevant distinction between killing and allowing to die, since the cause of death is different and the intention is very different, and both make a significant difference.

Proponents of PAS insist that there is nothing to worry about when it comes to legalizing PAS and how it might lead to a slippery slope. They cite the example in Oregon, where the number of people who have utilized the law is quite small, and PAS has been carefully regulated to prevent abuses. But opponents of PAS cite scenarios in Europe, where it has been legalized (or not prosecuted) for longer periods, and there is evidence of a movement from voluntary to nonvoluntary euthanasia. Opponents of PAS insist that without intolerable invasions of privacy, it is not possible for the state to enforce the condition that all PAS be voluntary. It is quite possible for coercive conversations to occur with elderly loved ones, and no one will ever know whether the patient has been coerced into signing a consent for PAS.

In addition, it is clear that legalizing PAS and euthanasia in some parts of the world is part of a larger agenda that has little to do with individual autonomy and the exercise of a right to die and more to do with eugenics and broader social change. As O'Neill suggests,

> Indeed today, to insist on the right to continue living despite the economic or environmental cost of one's life, despite the 'uselessness' of one's life in comparison with the lives of other, more able-bodied individuals—is surely regarded as immoral—after all, it sins against the new moralities of environmental awareness and generational responsibility.[4]

This cultural view of the elderly is quite a contrast to the Bible's insistence on the sanctity of life.

---

4. Ibid., xv.

CONCLUSION

In view of the erosion of respect for the intrinsic value of life, especially at the margins of life, we must affirm that all human life has inherent dignity, regardless of one's ability to function. This affirmation reflects the Bible's clear teaching that innocent human life is not to be taken and that culture has an obligation to care for the least among us—in fact, that's one of the moral measures of a culture. However, this does not mean that medicine must use all available technology and treatments to keep all people alive at all times and at all costs. Patients can be theologically consistent and say "enough" to medicine when treatments are futile or are more burdensome than beneficial. But the sanctity of life is inconsistent with both suicide (whether medically assisted or not) and euthanasia.

Since we all will face the end of life at some point, and may have our loved ones making decisions for us should we lose the capacity to make those decisions for ourselves, it is wise to think about your wishes for end-of-life care—what you want and don't want and under what conditions—and to communicate them to your loved ones and put them in writing in an advance directive. Our hope is to model approaching death and dying with a Christian worldview which maintains that death is a conquered enemy and that we have resurrection and eternity to anticipate.

Review Questions

1. What do patients and family members need in the way of emotional and spiritual support when walking through the end of life?
2. Under what conditions is it acceptable to say "stop" to medicine?
3. How would you distinguish between killing and allowing to die?
4. How would you respond to the person who says, "I have a fundamental right to die whenever and however I choose"?

For Further Reading

Callahan, Daniel. *The Troubled Dream of Life: Living with Mortality.* New York: Simon and Schuster, 1993.

Chamberlain, Paul. *Final Wishes: A Cautionary Tale on Death, Dignity and Physician-Assisted Suicide.* Downers Grove, Ill.: InterVarsity Press, 2000.

Yuill, Kevin. *Assisted Suicide: The Liberal, Humanist Case against Legalization.* London: Palgrave Macmillan, 2013.

CHAPTER 9

CAPITAL PUNISHMENT

*Isn't the death penalty a barbaric holdover
that should be done away with today?*

A few years ago, I spent my summer vacation on jury duty, as the foreman of the jury in a homicide trial. After the predictable complaining about jury service, we recognized that our service was a serious responsibility, because we jury members held the fate of the defendant in our hands. We convicted the accused of manslaughter, a lesser charge than murder, because given the facts of the case, it was the only verdict the law would allow. We were not involved in the sentencing phase, but we all expected that the defendant would serve substantial jail time. Though this was not a death penalty case, it was a sobering experience because of the impact our decision had on the defendant's life. Had it been a capital case, in which the jury would also have decided on the penalty, having the death penalty as an option would have considerably magnified the pressure we felt.

Put yourself on a jury in a first-degree murder trial. Assume that the trial takes place in a jurisdiction that allows the death penalty, and that the facts of the case meet the legal requirements for the death penalty to be considered. Further assume that there is no doubt about the guilt of the defendant. You can even assume that the murder was captured on surveillance cameras that clearly identify the defendant, and that DNA evidence at the scene verifies the guilt of the accused. In addition, you can also assume that there is a diverse makeup of the jury, representative of the community in which the crime was committed. The jury is now in the penalty phase of the trial, and you must decide whether to impose the death penalty or life in prison without the possibility of parole. The law allows for the death penalty but does not mandate it. How do you feel about sentencing this defendant to death? How should you think about the death penalty from a Christian worldview?

Though most Western nations have outlawed capital punishment (CP), many states in the US still allow it, and it is still practiced in some parts of the developing world. In the mid-1970s, the US Supreme Court ruled that the death penalty did not necessarily constitute cruel and unusual punishment. Some US states currently have a moratorium on death sentences, so that investigations into suspected mistakes and abuses can be addressed.

People who favor CP are generally known as *retentionists*, while those who oppose it are called *abolitionists*. A person who believes CP is inherently wrong, in principle, is known as a *principled abolitionist*. There are some who are not opposed to CP in principle but have significant procedural reservations about how the death penalty is carried out. We will refer to a person who holds this view as the *procedural abolitionist*, considering him or her an abolitionist for all practical purposes. However, the seriousness of these procedural reservations exists on a continuum and might not make the person a total abolitionist. The person who holds this view might allow for CP in cases of serial killers or terrorists, for example.

THE BIBLE AND THE DEATH PENALTY

Capital punishment was practiced in biblical times, in both Old and New Testament eras. The OT allowed (some would argue, mandated) CP for a variety of offenses, such as premeditated murder (Ex. 21:12–14) and sexual offenses such as adultery (Lev. 20:10–21), incest (Lev. 20:11–12), bestiality (Ex. 22:19; Lev. 20:15–16), and sexual assault (Deut. 22:23–27). CP was also allowed for kidnapping (Ex. 21:16) and for religious offenses such as witchcraft (Ex. 22:18), human sacrifice (Lev. 20:2), idolatry (Ex. 22:20), and blasphemy (Lev. 24:11–14).

In the NT, there is little mention of CP, since under Roman rule, Israel did not have legal authority to impose death sentences.

The Mosaic law, which contains most of the Bible's references to CP, is no longer directly applicable to the church today, since followers of Jesus are no longer under the law (Rom. 6:14; 7:1–6). Neither is the culture a theocracy in which the law of God is automatically the law of the land. Though the OT law does teach CP for a variety of offenses, very few people hold that the church is bound to all of the law today, as OT Israel was. So the value of the OT law for the debate over CP is to suggest that there is nothing intrinsically wrong with CP, since God commanded it for certain crimes in the OT law. But whether it is allowed, or required, today is not a question the OT law by itself can answer for us.

However, not all of the OT teaching on CP is in the law of Moses. *Prior* to the law, in Genesis 9:5–6, the "life for life" principle is given, connected to the notion that human beings are made in the image of God. Genesis 9:6 states, "Whoever sheds human blood, by humans shall their blood be shed; for in the image of God has God made mankind." This is a stronger bit of biblical teaching on CP, since the "life for life" principle is linked to a universal theological truth—the image of God in human beings. Further, since it precedes the giving of the law, it is not subject to the theological limitations of the law discussed above. The Genesis text seems to be highlighting the inestimable, intrinsic value of human life by putting forth the strongest possible penalty for taking innocent human life. This passage suggests that there is nothing intrinsically unjust about the general principle of life for life in cases of premeditated murder. For other types of killing, such as accidental killing, self-defense, or killing in a just war, the "life for life" principle did not apply.

One final OT text relevant to CP is Numbers 35:30, which mandates that at least two eyewitnesses must testify against the accused. The underlying principle here is that prior to a death sentence, the certainty of guilt must be established. With sophisticated forensic evidence available today, the certainty of guilt can be established without eyewitnesses. In OT times, there was no better way to insure that the accused was guilty, and thus for such a serious penalty, the most reliable means of determining guilt was required. That's not necessarily true today; thus the specific OT cultural application (multiple eyewitnesses) of the general principle (the certainty of guilt) is not required.

In the NT, there are scant references to CP. Paul makes allusions to CP in some of his trial speeches (Acts 25:11) and alludes to CP in Romans 13:4, with his statement that the state does not "bear the sword for no reason"—at least a reference to criminal justice in general and possibly to CP in specific. Some have suggested that Jesus's teaching in the Sermon on the Mount (Matt. 5–7), specifically his mandate to turn the other cheek and love our enemies (Matt. 5:38–48), is a statement against CP. Further, in the account of the woman caught in adultery (John 8), Jesus mandates forgiveness when the law would have required CP. Neither of these texts is relevant to the debate over CP. The Sermon on the Mount is not for the state but for individuals in community. Romans 13:1–7 outlines the mandate for the state to punish and deter crime, not forgive it. In addition, the reason why Jesus released the woman caught in adultery was because it was an obvious setup to trap him, the evidence for which is the absence of the guilty man in the arrangement. So the NT evidence for CP is not abundant. At the least, it would seem that Genesis 9:5–6 allows for CP in principle, but with modest NT evidence supporting it.

PROCEDURAL ISSUES WITH THE DEATH PENALTY

Many of the issues with CP today have to do with how it's administered, as opposed to the principle of it. Though many abolitionists agree that the death penalty is wrong in principle, because they consider it a barbaric holdover from less enlightened times, most of the serious objections to CP are procedural. Not that this makes them any less important, only that they are a different sort of objection.

These procedural problems put some people in the place of being an abolitionist, for all practical purposes. They may accept the death penalty in principle but argue that there are such significant procedural issues that it renders them an abolitionist. Of course, retentionists can also have concerns about CP based on these objections, and it may limit the kinds of cases for which they would be willing to consider CP a moral option.

Though not a procedural point, many abolitionists consider the death penalty to be a double message about the sanctity of life. They argue that CP undermines the state's upholding life's inherent value. Abolitionists insist that the right to life is inalienable, that it cannot be taken away or forfeited. Retentionists respond by insisting that the sanctity of life is focused on innocent life. They argue that the right to life is inalienable not in an absolute sense but only without due process of law, according to the Constitution. That is, one's right to life can be forfeited by taking another's, but not without full and fair due process of law. The principled abolitionist will generally insist that the right to life is inalienable, with or without due process, making it unjust to ever take human life. Principled abolitionists are usually pacifists about the morality of war and even about using violence in self-defense.

Abolitionists are also concerned about mistakes being made and undeserving people being executed. They point out that with the advent of new forensic technology such as DNA evidence, some people on death row awaiting execution have been shown to be innocent of the crimes they were convicted of. Some states in the US, such as Illinois and New Jersey, have put a moratorium on death sentences until they fully understand why these mistakes are made. Given these exonerations, it would be naive to assume that mistakes have not been made in the past and that innocent men and women have not been executed mistakenly. It is true that people are wrongly imprisoned in justice systems around the world, but these people can be released and can be compensated for the mistakes made, neither of which can be done with erroneous executions.

Abolitionists argue that regardless of the level of forensic technology, fallible human beings are still involved in the criminal justice system, and mistakes not only are possible but in fact are inevitable in such a system. This is more acute in parts of the world where criminal justice is carried out by judges or other government officials, as opposed to a jury of one's peers. One of my former students, who came to study with us from the Philippines, commented that in her hometown, judges—who in her view were easily corruptible—handled sentencing, including death sentences. As a result, this procedural issue made her a complete abolitionist, though she had no problem with CP in principle.

Related to this objection that mistakes can be and are made is another issue about which both believers and the nonreligious care deeply. They cite the evidence of death row prisoners reforming their lives, becoming different people and committing themselves to being contributing members of society. For many of these people, the reason for the change in their lives and outlook is a religious conversion, either to Christianity or, increasingly in recent years, to Islam. The argument is that execution both cuts off this opportunity for redemption and life change and seems like a waste of someone's potential for future contribution to society. To put it in distinctly Christian terms, CP removes the possibility of the person coming to faith in Christ.

Retentionists respond that the appeal process, which takes years (the average stay on death row in California is twenty years), allows sufficient time for someone to experience redemption. They further argue that there are few pressures in life as compelling as impending mortality to encourage someone to get their life in order. Theologically, God's sovereign role in men and women coming to faith cannot be undermined by any human activity, including the death penalty, though it does seem like a waste of a redeemed life to proceed with execution. But retentionists insist that justice and redemption are separate issues, and they cite the stories of death row inmates such as Karla Faye Tucker, who genuinely came to faith in Christ while on death row and never requested a stay of execution, recognizing that justice for her crimes was unrelated to her redeemed life. Though our intuitions tell us that the loss of her future contribution to society was squandered, it may also be that if reform or redemption were a condition for avoiding CP, virtually everyone would opt for a death row conversion.

Abolitionists are also concerned about the discriminatory way in which CP is applied. The majority of executions are of African American and Hispanic males. It is very rare for a woman to face a death sentence, and white males get death sentences less frequently than minority men, even when taking into account the incidence of violent crimes committed. Abolitionists argue that this reflects an inherent racial bias in the criminal justice system, a notion that has been reinforced by well-publicized police shootings of minority men. Abolitionists insist that given current racial biases in society, CP cannot be administered in a just fashion.

Retentionists maintain that the injustice is not that minority men receive the death penalty but that nonminority defendants are given life terms when CP is deserved. They further argue that the existence of bias does not necessarily compel the criminal justice system to abandon CP, any more than bias means that other types of sentencing cannot occur. Nonetheless, both sides acknowledge that, at least in some communities, racial and ethnic bias does exist and has made a difference in the administration of CP, though there is ongoing debate about the degree to which that taints the death penalty.

CONCLUSION

Though the death penalty has been abolished in most of the Western world, it still exists in parts of the developing world and some states in the US. The biblical material on CP, especially in the NT, leaves some people feeling that the Bible is not clear enough to be determinative on this issue. Though the part of the Bible that has the most to say about CP—the Mosaic law—is not directly addressed to the present day, it is relevant in that it reinforces the general principle of life for life laid out in Genesis 9:5–6. This presents a challenge to the principled abolitionist, who holds that there is something inherently immoral about CP. However, the procedural issues that have been raised, particularly the possibility (some would argue the inevitability) of mistakes being made, and the discriminatory application of CP, both suggest at the least that significant limits be placed on its administration. At most, these issues could understandably make someone a procedural abolitionist.

There are hard questions for both retentionists and abolitionists to answer about their position. For the abolitionist, addressing Genesis 9:5–6 remains a problem. It underlies a further hard question for the abolitionist: what is intrinsically unjust about the principle of life for life? Why does someone not forfeit their life when they take another innocent life in premeditated fashion?

For the retentionist, the hard question is that, given that mistakes will be made, what exactly is lost when first-degree murder is punished with a life sentence without parole? It may be that in many cases the answer is, not very much, though prosecutors will argue that having the death penalty available makes it easier for them to deliver plea bargains by being able to take it off the table in exchange for guilty pleas to lesser crimes. They may also argue that without the death penalty, the deterrent value of CP is lost, though the murder rate is influenced by many factors, and isolating CP from those other factors is difficult if not impossible. And it may be that with no death penalty, a sense of justice is not served in some egregious cases of murder, such as mass murder and terrorism. But it may also be that in many cases of murder for which CP would be considered, there is no great loss with a life term, especially not one that would offset the gain of being assured that the criminal justice system does not wrongly execute anyone.

Review Questions

1. If you were on a jury in a capital murder case for which the death penalty was an option, how would you vote?
2. What are some of the places in the Bible that address the death penalty? How do those texts help form your view of capital punishment?
3. How do you respond to the statement that capital punishment is a cruel and barbaric holdover from ancient times and has no place in a civilized society?
4. Summarize the arguments in favor of and opposed to the death penalty.

For Further Reading

Budziszewski, J., E. J. Dionne, Avery Cardinal Dulles, and Stanley Hauerwas. *Religion and the Death Penalty: A Call for Reckoning.* Grand Rapids: Eerdmans, 2004.

CHAPTER 10

WAR AND MORALITY

In view of the Bible's teaching to love your enemies, why isn't every Christian a pacifist?

Think back to your history classes in high school, and recall the times you studied the major wars that shaped the history of the part of the world in which you grew up. Consider World Wars I and II, and more recently, for US citizens, the Vietnam War in the 1960s and the war in Iraq in the 2000s. If you come from the non-Western world, think about the wars that are prominent in your history. Then ask yourself this: given your convictions, which if any of these wars could you, in good conscience, participate in as a combatant? Think specifically about the reasons why you either could or could not serve in a combatant role.

An exercise like this should help sharpen your view of the morality of war. If your answer to all wars is that you could not participate for any reason, you likely hold a view known as *pacifism*. But if you could participate in at least some of the wars, you probably espouse a view known as *just war theory*. You hold that there is such a thing as a just war, and your decision about participation depends on meeting specific criteria for what constitutes a just war.

Pacifism today has two primary versions. The first is called *nonviolent pacifism*, and the second is known as *nonparticipatory pacifism*. The difference between the two is the degree of cooperation with the use of violence necessary for participation as a combatant. The nonviolent pacifist is morally opposed to the use of violence, especially lethal violence under any circumstances, including war and personal self-defense. Nonparticipatory pacifism goes further, insisting that one cannot participate in support roles for war efforts either. Thus someone could not serve in the military in a support role or work for defense contractors who make weapons systems. Where one draws the line in this area varies widely, since many companies that support the military also provide goods and services to the civilian sector.

Similarly, the just war notion has several versions. *Traditional just war theory* maintains that a just war is strictly one of self-defense against an imminent threat. But extensions of the just war doctrine can include *preemptive strikes*, given an enemy's impending attack, and *wars that either prevent or reverse injustices*. Examples of the preemptive strike include Israel's attack on the Arab nations in the Six-Day War in 1967. Wars to reverse or prevent injustice are most clearly seen when a nation intervenes to prevent another from engaging in genocide, as has been the case periodically, and most recently, in Africa.

The OT contains accounts of a variety of armed conflicts between Israel and their neighbors. There are examples of preventive strikes (2 Sam. 11:1), wars of aggression (Josh. 1–8 in taking the Promised Land), wars of self-defense, and even what is called putting nations "under the ban," which involved their total annihilation. In the NT, with the nation of Israel and the church both being persecuted minorities, there was a general spirit of pacifism, and the early followers of Jesus refrained from using violence in self-defense against their persecutors, even to the point of martyrdom in some cases.

It would have been unusual for the early believers to serve in the military, since it was the primary agent of persecution against the early church and involved taking an oath of loyalty to Caesar that violated their faith in Jesus as their Lord. However, in several examples in the Gospels when soldiers come to faith in Jesus, they are not required to give up their profession as a condition of following Jesus faithfully (Matt. 8:5–13; Acts 10:1–48). The most striking example of this is when soldiers are converted through the preaching of John the Baptist, and they specifically ask what they must do as a result of their repentance. John replies, "Don't extort money and don't accuse people falsely—be content with your pay" (Luke 3:14). That is, they were not to abuse their power as soldiers to exact unfair benefits or be involved in injustice, but it was not required that they give up their military profession.

PACIFISM AND THE BIBLE

The main portions of the Bible that address the morality of war and pacifism include Jesus's teaching about loving your enemies in the Sermon on the Mount (Matt. 5:38–48), Paul's teaching on not repaying evil for evil (Rom. 12:17–21), and Peter's admonition to follow the nonviolent example of Christ on the cross (1 Peter 2:18–24).

The most common point of biblical reference for pacifism comes from Jesus's teaching in Matthew 5, with the admonitions not to resist an evil person (v. 39) and to love your enemies (v. 44). Pacifists insist that faithfully following Jesus involves a commitment to forego the use of violence under all circumstances when confronted by evil. For example, philosopher Robert Brimlow, in his book *What about Hitler?* concludes that when faced with evil such as that which Nazi Germany brought in WWII, the authentic Christian response is as follows:

> We must live faithfully; we must be humble in our faith and truthful in what we say and do; we must repay evil with good; and we must be peacemakers. This may also mean as a result that evildoers will kill us. Then, we also shall die. That's it. There is nothing else—or rather anything else is only a footnote to this. We are called to live the kingdom as he proclaimed it and be his disciples, come what may.[1]

---

1. Robert Brimlow, *What about Hitler? Wrestling with Jesus' Call to Nonviolence in an Evil World* (Grand Rapids: Brazos Press, 2006), 151.

He ultimately concludes that faithfulness to Jesus is more important than defending oneself against evil, even if it means one's death. Brimlow puts it this way: "Our call to follow Jesus and be peacemakers means that we will die. We don't like this message, so we recoil from it and consider it incomprehensible; and we find ways to reinterpret the gospel or to understand the 'real' meaning of Jesus' message in order to obfuscate and avoid this conclusion."[2]

Some pacifists distinguish between nonresistance to evil and nonviolence in the face of evil. For example, Martin Luther King Jr. was well known as a pacifist but nonetheless engaged in nonviolent resistance to people who were denying civil rights to African Americans.

Just war advocates maintain that Jesus's teaching on nonresistance to evil in the Sermon on the Mount does not apply to situations in which there is a mortal threat to a person or group. They insist that the command to avoid resisting an evil person (Matt. 5:39) is qualified by the four illustrations that follow—turning the other cheek, going the extra mile, giving your coat as well as your shirt, and lending to people who want to borrow. They argue that these are insults and humiliations, not life-threatening situations.

Further, when Jesus says to turn the other cheek, for example, they suggest that he is not stating a literal requirement but rather using a figure of speech to indicate that a believer should refrain from the natural reaction to strike back. Thus Jesus is teaching *nonretaliation*, not the avoidance of self-defense or defense of others when life is threatened. They insist that the mandate to love your enemies occurs in this context, of personal humiliations and persecutions, not in the context of life-threatening danger.

Similarly, pacifists argue that in Romans 12:17–21, Paul is teaching that we are never to return evil for evil (v. 17) and that followers of Jesus are to overcome evil with good (v. 21). They insist that the use of violence, especially lethal force, is always evil and

---

2. Ibid., 167.

must be avoided, regardless of the threat. But just war advocates maintain that Paul is clearly addressing nonretaliation in this passage (v. 19) and that repaying evil for evil (v. 17) is addressing revenge, not self-defense, since it is about *repaying* evil with evil. Thus, instead of retaliation, the believer is to do good to his or her enemies. The just war advocate argues that this text precludes only retaliation, not self-defense. This is also the structure of the original OT mandate to love your neighbor, which is set opposite the prohibition on seeking revenge and holding grudges (Lev. 19:18). Thus the opposite of loving one's neighbor is retaliation, not self-defense.

Referring to 1 Peter 2:18–24, pacifists argue that the nonviolent example of Christ on the cross is the paradigm for the believer's nonviolent response to evil, even if it's a life-threatening situation, as it was for Jesus. They point out that the text specifically holds that Jesus's example of suffering for doing good is one that all of his followers should imitate (vv. 20–21). The just war advocate points out that the specific example of Jesus's behavior cited in verse 23 ("When they hurled their insults at him, he did not retaliate; when he suffered, he made no threats") suggests nonretaliation, consistent with the other primary texts that pacifists claim support their view.

Just war advocates point out that the notion of loving your neighbor supports the use of force if necessary. Saint Augustine posed the scenario in which you come across someone being beaten and about to be killed, and argues that if you stand idly by and allow the person to be beaten and killed, you cannot maintain that you are loving your neighbor. Retaliation is never allowed, consistent with the teaching of Jesus, Paul, and Peter, but the mandate to love your neighbor can be consistent with using force, even lethal force if necessary, to repel the attack.

The advocates argue further that if the state is mandated to use force to protect its inhabitants and insure order and justice, according to Romans 13:1–7, then there is no reason why believers cannot cooperate with the state in the discharge of its God-ordained responsibilities. This would include military service in just wars as well as law enforcement. As we suggested in the discussion on capital punishment, the Sermon on the Mount applies to the individual facing humiliation and persecution, not to the state in its role of enforcing order and justice.

THE JUST WAR TRADITION

The just war tradition, though it began and took shape in the context of Christianity, has become the primary way in which most of the West has viewed the intersection of war and morality. Much of the secularized West still uses the just war criteria to determine whether entering an armed conflict is morally appropriate. For example, in much of the public discussion, even in the media, surrounding the decision to go to war in Iraq in 2003, the categories of the just war were regularly invoked.

The roots of the just war tradition come from the teachings of Augustine in the early days of church history. Augustine envisioned a hypothetical situation in which person A encounters person B being beaten by person C to the point that if person A does not intervene, person B will likely be killed by person C. Augustine then argued that if person A stands idly by and allows person B to be maimed or killed, person A cannot say that he has been faithful to Jesus's command to love his neighbor. That is, the mandate to love your neighbor as yourself (Luke 10:27, reflecting Lev. 19:18) involves rescuing your neighbor from harm and using force, even lethal force if necessary, to repel the attack.

Just war advocates further argue that the mandate to love your neighbor *as yourself* also justifies personal self-defense, not simply intervention to protect others. This would open the door to personal self-defense, as well as involvement in military service and law enforcement. Given the role of the state in Romans 13:1–7, which allows for the use of force by the state in its God-ordained responsibility to protect its citizens, insure order, and promote justice, the believer then would be justified in participating with the state in the administration of its divinely mandated duty. The just war advocate would not hold that the use of force is necessarily inconsistent with faithfully following Jesus, but would hold that under the right conditions, both war and violence could be justified.

The original just war formulation maintained that the use of force, even lethal force, was not necessarily evil but could be a moral good under the proper conditions. The formulation maintained a similar position about war, that it was not necessarily evil but could be a morally good thing if exercised according to the just war criteria. The same could be said of law enforcement. This is a sharp contrast to the way the just war tradition is articulated today, in which war is evil but can be justified as a necessary evil under the just war criteria.

Given the devastation of war and the harm caused by the use of violence, the specific criteria for its use are very important. The just war criteria include the *jus ad bello* criteria (referring to justice in the decision to go to war) and the *jus in bello* criteria (referring to justice in the conduct of war). All criteria must be met for a war to be considered just, and a violation of any of the criteria is sufficient to render a war unjust.

The *jus ad bello* criteria, regarding the decision to go to war, include the following:

1. *Just cause*, which is the need to deal with legitimate and imminent threats that require self-defense, though just causes can also include preemptive strikes and either preventing or reversing clear injustices.
2. *Just intention*, which is the goal of securing a fair peace for all parties involved.
3. *Last resort*, which means that all other avenues for pursuing a peaceful resolution of the conflict have been exhausted.
4. *Formal declaration by properly constituted authorities*, which means that the conduct of war is the prerogative of governments, not individuals, vigilante groups, or paramilitary units operating outside legitimate government authority.

When it comes to conduct in war, the *jus in bello* criteria include:

1. *Limited objectives*, meaning that the overriding purpose for a just war is peace, not the humiliation and economic crippling of another nation.
2. *Proportionate means*, which suggests that the amount of force used must be proportionate to the threat. Only force sufficient to repel and deter the aggressor can be justifiably used.
3. *Noncombatant immunity*, which means that only combatants may be targeted by the enemy. Civilians, wounded soldiers, and prisoners of war cannot be objects of attack. This final category does distinguish between targeting noncombatants and what is known as "collateral damage," in which noncombatants might be killed or injured but they are not the intended target of the attack. However, both terrorism and the use of nuclear weapons would violate this last criterion, since they both specifically and intentionally target civilians.

Though some have suggested that the just war criteria have been rendered obsolete by modern military technology, the criteria have been remarkably durable over the centuries and, outside of pacifism, remain the standard framework for viewing the morality of war.

The most recent ethical debate in the conduct of the war on terrorism has to do with the morality of the use of torture. The just war idea as well as the notion of basic human rights, operating on a deontological foundation of the principle of intrinsic human dignity, insists that torture is immoral and should not be used, since it violates the inherent dignity of the prisoner of war. Critics of this view construct a scenario in which a captive has critical information that must be obtained in order to save many lives.

Operating within a utilitarian framework, one could argue that the benefits could be so substantial in terms of lives saved that torture of a prisoner of war could be justified. The greater the benefit, the more likely torture could be justified from a utilitarian perspective. For example, if torture were to gain information that would save an entire city from being destroyed, it is not difficult to imagine the justification for use of torture in that setting. The opponent of torture would insist that no utilitarian calculus can justify something as intrinsically repulsive, from a deontological view, as torture. Though there may be some debate about the definition of torture—as some distinguish it from what they call "extreme measures," such as sleep deprivation, solitary confinement, sensory denial, and other forms of discomfort—the opponents of torture would insist that genuine torture is always unethical because of its assault on human dignity.

The contemporary discussion regarding torture involves the specific technique known as "waterboarding," which simulates drowning, and some would insist it is actually subjecting someone to drowning and is not a simulation at all. The consensus seems to be that it does constitute torture, but it is part of training for special forces, and some journalists have volunteered to undergo it as a test to see if it constitutes torture. To some people, this seems to suggest that it is more of an extreme measure, since no one would voluntarily undergo the more traditional forms of torture, which leave permanent physical damage.

CONCLUSION

Jesus predicted that wars and rumors of wars will be with us until his second coming. With the continued rise of global terrorism, questions of the morality of war, both in its initiation and in its conduct, will be relevant for some time to come. Thus the age-old debate between pacifists and advocates of the just war will likely remain until Christ, the Prince of Peace, returns and brings a real and lasting peace. The prophet Isaiah predicted this final, universal peace in vivid terms: "They will beat their swords into plowshares and their spears into pruning hooks. Nation will not take up sword against nation, nor will they train for war anymore" (Isa. 2:4).

Review Questions

1. What are the various types of wars presented in the Old Testament?
2. Do you believe that the Bible mandates pacifism? Why or why not?
3. What are the various types of just wars according to just war proponents?
4. What are the criteria for a just war according to just war proponents?
5. What do you think about the use of torture when its use could uncover information that would save lives?

For Further Reading

Brimlow, Robert W. *What about Hitler? Wrestling with Jesus' Call to Nonviolence in an Evil World.* Grand Rapids: Brazos Press, 2006.

Charles, J. Daryl. *Between Pacifism and Jihad: Just War and Christian Tradition.* Downers Grove, Ill.: InterVarsity Press, 2005.

CHAPTER 11

SEXUAL ETHICS

Shouldn't people be able to love and have sex with whomever they choose?

Few areas of culture have been changing faster than the area of sex and sexuality. For example, in 2004, voters in California approved Proposition 8, maintaining that marriage is between one man and one woman. Only eleven years later, the US Supreme Court ruled that same-sex marriage is a constitutional right. Within weeks of that decision, other types of marital arrangements were being proposed, from polyamory (multiple marriage), to marriage to blood relatives, to bestiality (marriage to animals). In addition, today we live in the midst of a "hookup" culture in which sex is increasingly divorced from meaningful relationships. Further, public institutions are addressing not only same-sex relationships, but also transgender issues, as the recent sex change of Olympian Bruce Jenner illustrates. These all have their roots in the soil of a culture of autonomy, in which individual rights and entitlements are seen as primary, and where the satisfaction of one's desires is a top priority.

Consider the following scenarios and think about how you would respond to the person in each one.

> A high school student comes to you with questions about his or her sexual orientation, as he or she realizes that the only sexual attraction felt is toward the same sex. Imagine this scenario if the student in question were your child.

A young adult considers himself female, though he is anatomically male, and is considering a sex change.

A college-age heterosexual couple who have been dating for some time and considering marriage ask you, what's the big deal about waiting until marriage for sex? They insist that nobody waits until marriage today.

A high school girl comes to you for advice and tells you that she believes the only way she can hold a guy's interest in her is to have sex with him, even though she doesn't feel ready for sex.

A woman in her late thirties expresses disappointment that her church is putting pressure on her to get married and have kids before her biological clock runs out.

Your sister comes to you and invites you to her wedding to her lesbian partner. (Or consider that she requests that you perform the ceremony.)

These are only a sample of the sexual ethics issues encountered today. Though this chapter could easily encompass an entire book, after putting sexual ethics in its biblical context, we will limit our discussion to the following areas: singleness and celibacy, birth control, homosexuality and same-sex marriage, and transgender issues.

THE BIBLE AND SEXUALITY

The Bible has a great deal to say about sex and sexuality. As my graduate school mentor put it, "When God spoke about sex, he didn't stutter!" The Bible's teaching is clear and unequivocal about the importance of sexual purity and avoiding sexual immorality (1 Thess. 4:3–6; 1 Cor. 6:18). The reason why this is so important is that sexual immorality violates a person's relationship with all three members of the Trinity. In 1 Corinthians 6:12–20, it's clear that sexual immorality is a sin against God the Father, who will raise the body from the dead (v. 14). It is further a sin against God the Son, in that since we are united with Christ, we join Christ to the other person with whom the sexual sin takes place (vv. 15–17). Moreover, it is a sin against God the Holy Spirit, since our bodies are temples of the Holy Spirit (v. 19). The person committed to following Christ is to honor God with the body, emphasizing the importance of the physical side of life.

There's widespread agreement in the Christian community that sexual immorality is to be avoided, but what's under debate today is the question, what constitutes sexual immorality? Some people suggest that monogamous, committed same-sex relationships do not constitute immorality,[1] nor does premarital sex between two heterosexual people committed to each other.

The Bible's teaching on sexuality begins at the beginning of the biblical narrative in Genesis 1–2. As developed in chapter 6 of this book, regarding reproductive technology, the Genesis account of creation teaches that sex and procreation both flourish best when practiced within permanent, monogamous, heterosexual marriage. Genesis 2:24 summarizes this when it indicates that a man shall leave his father and mother (a public, ceremonial leaving), be united to his wife, and then the two shall become one flesh (referring to the sexual consummation of marriage). This is echoed in the only book of the Bible that directly addresses sex in marriage—Song of Songs. There the book proceeds from getting acquainted to courtship (1:1–3:5), to the marriage ceremony (3:6–10), and then to the wedding night (4:1–5:1), and it's intended that this order is the norm.

The prophets who refer to idolatry as "spiritual adultery" reinforce the marriage setting as the place for sexual relations (Hos. 2:2–13; 4:15). The Mosaic law further clarifies this foundation by allowing for sexual relations within heterosexual marriage and prohibiting all forms of sexual relationships outside that setting (Lev. 18:1–29; 20:10–21). The law rules out adultery, homosexual

---

1. See, for example, David P. Gushee, *Changing Our Mind: A Call from America's Leading Ethics Scholar for Full Acceptance of LGBT Christians in the Church* (Nashville: David Crumm Media, 2015).

sex, incest of various forms, and bestiality (sex with animals). The law, intending to safeguard the sanctity of marriage, sets boundaries around sexual expression, limiting it to heterosexual marriage.

In addition to protecting marriage, a further reason for these prohibitions was to enable Israel to avoid the idolatrous religious practices of its neighbors, who regularly engaged in religious prostitution as a part of their worship. The Wisdom Literature of the OT celebrates the beauty of sex within marriage (Song of Songs; Prov. 5:15–17) but also warns of the seduction of adultery and prostitution (Prov. 5–6). The NT routinely cautions the believer about succumbing to the temptations of sexual immorality generally, using the Greek term *porneia*, which is the general term for all forms of sexual activity outside of heterosexual marriage (Mark 7:21; Acts 15:20; Rom. 13:13; Eph. 5:3; Col. 3:5). More specifically, the NT indicates that homosexual sex is outside the boundaries of morally legitimate sexual relations (Rom. 1:24–27; 1 Cor. 6:9–11).

MARRIAGE AND SINGLENESS

A few years ago, for the first time, the US census indicated that households headed by single adults outnumbered those headed by married couples. There is less emphasis on marriage today as the number of couples cohabiting continues to rise and more adults choose not to remarry after divorce. The "married with children" model is no longer the predominant one culturally, and as a result, the number of single adults in our churches is higher than ever.

This sometimes raises tensions for family-oriented churches, especially in cultures that strongly emphasize marriage and children. This emphasis often leaves single adults feeling like second-class citizens in their churches, as the ideal of marriage and family continues to be the expectation. This stands in contrast to what the Bible emphasizes—that what makes a person complete *is being in Christ* (Col. 2:10), not being married.

The Bible addresses the subject of singleness directly in one specific place in the NT, in 1 Corinthians 7:25–38. The apostle Paul was very qualified to write on this, since he was likely once married and now single at the time of the writing of 1 Corinthians. Remember that Paul was a member of the Jewish Sanhedrin, or ruling elders, before his conversion to Christ. It would have been very unlikely for him to have been a member of the Sanhedrin and to not have been married. But it seems clear that he's writing as a single person in the epistles of the NT. The most plausible explanation for his change of status is that his wife left him after his conversion, though we are not told anywhere in his letters about any further details.

First Corinthians 7:25–38 makes the point that neither marriage nor singleness is inherently superior to the other, and under some circumstances, singleness is the most expedient alternative. He gives three reasons why this is so. First, he maintains that as a result of the "present crisis," singleness may be the more advisable option (v. 26). The "present crisis" refers to the context of persecution that the Corinthian church was facing. In this situation, in which one is likely to face intense persecution, having a wife and children makes one more vulnerable to the pressure of persecution. Though this might not be the case in most of the West, if someone is pursuing a job or service opportunity in parts of the world where the church is persecuted, this is still good advice today. However, Paul makes it clear that if someone chooses to marry, even in these challenging circumstances, that too is morally acceptable.

Paul's second reason supporting the notion of marriage and singleness being morally equivalent is not circumstantial but intrinsic. He argues that in view of the imminent return of Christ and how the present form of this world is passing away (vv. 29–31), marriage is not eternal. In fact, in the eternal state, the church will be united with Christ, using the metaphor of bride and bridegroom. Since marriage is not eternal, it can't be morally superior to singleness.

His third reason appears at first glance to be circumstantial but is actually an argument for the intrinsic equality of marriage and singleness. Paul speaks of marriage bringing divided loyalties for both men and women—divided, that is, between pleasing God and pleasing one's spouse (vv. 32–35). A single person has more ability to live in undivided devotion to Christ (v. 35), and that seems to be just as true today as in the first century. But that being so, how does anyone justify a decision to get married? Paul again affirms that the decision to get married or remain single, in and of itself, is not morally problematic; both are acceptable to God (vv. 36–38). Part of the answer to this would be to consider the kingdom reasons for getting married—for example, that as a couple, you could serve the kingdom more effectively than by being single. This seems to be an important part of any Christian couple's decision about marriage and makes the decision about more than love and not living without the other person.

The application of this to the church is to suggest that marriage does not complete a person, nor does marriage represent a destination. Rather marriage is getting a traveling companion for the journey of life. In many cultures, a person is considered to have arrived once married. But for most in healthy marriages, in which the relationship shapes their character, marriage only indicates how far one has to go before arriving at maturity. Single adults should be accepted and not regarded as having something missing in their lives because they are not married. Nor should the church oversell marriage, since marriage is essentially the union of two miserable, wretched, self-centered sinners! Jesus indicated that celibacy is a gift (Matt. 19:11), and singleness should be affirmed, not used as an occasion to regard brothers and sisters in Christ as second-class spiritual citizens.

BIRTH CONTROL

Except in official Roman Catholic circles, birth control is widely accepted, both culturally and in the Christian community. However, it's important to distinguish between birth control that is strictly contraceptive (prevents conception, such as condoms, sponges, spermicides) and that which is abortifacient (prevents implantation or expels a fertilized embryo out of the uterus, such as IUDs, Ella drugs). People who insist that all birth control is problematic often argue from the biblical texts that indicate that children are a gift and a blessing (Ps. 127:3–5) and that human beings, from creation to the present, are commanded to be fruitful and multiply (Gen. 1:28).

It is true that in the book of Genesis, God commanded human beings to procreate, the goal of which was to fill the earth, a goal which has been fulfilled, many times over. As a result, it would seem that the mandate to be fruitful and multiply is no longer in effect. It is also true that children are a blessing, though not in precisely the same way as in ancient times, since children were viewed as economic assets for parents in a largely agricultural society. However, children being a gift does not obligate parents to have as many children as they can. There is also a stewardship mandate that comes with the original dominion mandate in Genesis 1–2, which holds human beings accountable for responsible use of God's good gifts. The obligation for stewardship, both of the larger world and of the family's resources, as well as the ability of the mother and father to effectively parent only so many children, balances the idea of children as a gift.

Official Roman Catholic teaching prohibits artificial birth control (a rhythm method is acceptable), because the Catholic Church views sexual relations as consisting of a unitive and a procreative element, both of which must be present if sexual relations are to proceed as God designed. That is, the couple must be open to procreation every time they engage in sex. Thus one cannot separate the unitive and procreative aspects of sex, and therefore artificial birth control, abortion, and most reproductive technologies are prohibited.

However, the Bible seems to view the unitive, or "one flesh," aspect of sex as a sufficient end in itself, as Song of Songs exalts the pleasure and enjoyment of sex (the unitive element) with no mention of anything to do with procreation. Similarly, in 1 Corinthians 7:1–7, Paul recognizes the importance of regular marital sex as a protection against sexual immorality, so the couple won't look outside marriage to satisfy their unitive sexual desires. In addition, the onset of menopause for women would seem to be a natural and God-ordained separation of the unitive and procreative aspects of sex, as it is difficult to see how a couple could have an openness to procreation after menopause has set in.

If there is no mandate against birth control in general, then does the type of birth control matter? If the method is genuinely contraceptive, preventing egg and sperm from coming together, that is not problematic, since eggs and sperm are not the same as an embryo. But if the method is abortifacient, that's a different matter, since once fertilization has occurred, a person is in view. Methods that prevent implantation or expel an embryo from the womb are both problematic.

The most controversial form of birth control is the birth control pill. The hormones it contains can be taken orally, in a vaginal ring, or in longer-acting form under the skin. There is considerable debate over what exactly the pill does. Everyone agrees that its primary function is to prevent conception, by preventing ovulation. The debatable part is over what is commonly referred to as the "backup mechanism," which makes the uterus inhospitable for implantation. Some insist that this is part of the pill's design, and others argue that the pill is entirely contraceptive. The consensus at present seems to be that the pill does have this backup mechanism, and though it is difficult if not impossible to know how often the backup is needed, it does make the pill problematic.

HOMOSEXUALITY AND SAME-SEX MARRIAGE

With the controversial *Obergefell* decision of the US Supreme Court in mid-2015, which ruled that same-sex marriage is a constitutional right, cultural acceptance of homosexuality and same-sex marriage had significant momentum and placed culture on a collision course with historic, orthodox Christian ethics. Though some Christian denominations had previously recognized same-sex relationships as consistent with the teaching of the Bible, most within more evangelical circles maintained that same-sex relationships were at odds with the teaching of the Bible.[2]

As already mentioned, the Genesis account sets sexual relations firmly within the context of heterosexual marriage, and the Mosaic law, intending to protect that ideal, prohibits all other sexual relationships outside the Genesis norm. Homosexual relationships are not singled out among these but are mentioned as simply some of the relationships that are at odds with God's original design in Genesis. Other parts of the OT that refer to homosexuality include Genesis 19, the account of the destruction of Sodom and Gomorrah—which, homosexual proponents argue, does not apply to this discussion, since it describes and condemns *nonconsensual sex*. They further point out that when the prophets describe the sin of Sodom and Gomorrah, sex is not mentioned; what condemned the cities was their materialism and callousness to the poor among them (Ezek. 16:49). However, later NT commentary on this narrative refers to the rampant sexual immorality of all kinds in these cities as part of what led to their downfall (Jude 7).

The primary NT text that addresses homosexuality is Romans 1:18–32, the primary point of which is that all of humanity is under the condemnation of sin and thus in need of redemption, setting the stage for the message of Christ the Savior. The argument in this section is to show that homosexuality is one of the many manifestations of idolatry, as cultures give up belief in God for various forms of idolatry. The central part of the text (vv. 25–27) reads,

> They exchanged the truth about God for a lie, and worshiped and served created things rather than the Creator—who is forever praised. Amen. Because of this, God gave them

---

2. For exceptions to this, see Gushee, *Changing Our Minds*, and Matthew Vines, *God and the Gay Christian: The Biblical Case in Support of Same-Sex Relationships* (New York: Convergent, 2014).

over to shameful lusts. Even their women exchanged natural sexual relations for unnatural ones. In the same way the men also abandoned natural relations with women and were inflamed with lust for one another.

Advocates of homosexuality have a variety of ways of reading this central passage. Some insist that Paul is condemning homosexuality in the context of idolatry, that is, its occurrence in the idolatrous religious rituals of the time, which did include prostitution, with both same sex and opposite sex. Others argue that Paul is condemning sexual inversion, that is, someone having sex which is against their sexual nature, which would mean gay persons having heterosexual sex, and straight persons engaging in homosexual sex.

Still others maintain that Paul is condemning sexual excess, that is, engaging in homosexual sex in addition to having heterosexual sex with one's spouse. This view assumes that most men in first-century Greco-Roman culture were bisexual, and that to give up the sexual excess did not mean giving up sex entirely.

What these alternative interpretations have in common is the insistence that the passage is not addressing loving, monogamous same-sex relationships, and thus the Bible is not at odds with these kinds of same-sex relationships.

Other proponents of homosexuality argue from outside the text on broader grounds of how to interpret Paul's teaching in general. They maintain that Paul was reflecting his homophobic background and culture, and thus his teaching is unduly colored by his personal and cultural biases. They suggest that he does the same thing in his teaching on women, reflecting his patriarchal culture, by maintaining that men are to exercise leadership in the home and the church (1 Cor. 11:2–4; 14:34–35; 1 Tim. 2:11–14).

Proponents of the traditional view maintain that Romans 1 was intended as a universal statement on sexuality, consistent with the teaching of Genesis 1–2 and the Mosaic law. It fits with the consistent witness of the Bible that all sexual relationships outside the norm of heterosexual sex in marriage are outside of God's design. When Paul specifies that men "abandoned natural relations *with women*" (Rom. 1:27) for same-sex attraction and sex, he is identifying the natural sexual relation with heterosexuality. That is, the *natural* sexual relationship, between a man and a woman, is natural in an objective, not subjective, sense.

Traditional proponents further insist that Paul is actually quite countercultural in his teaching. The assumption that he was captive to his homophobic culture might have some weight if his teaching were written to the Jews of his time, but Paul's central teaching on homosexuality was written to the Romans, and previously to the Corinthians, both cities being examples of a sexual cornucopia, parallel to most major metropolitan areas of the world today. If anything, Paul was teaching something quite out of step with the cultures in which he found himself.

In order to apply the NT teaching correctly, it's very important to distinguish between sexual *orientation* and sexual *behavior*. The NT texts in view prohibit the behavior, not the orientation. The emphasis is on preventing sexual lust and any additional sexual behavior outside heterosexual marriage. As a result, it is entirely possible for a person to have a same-sex orientation and still act in accordance with the general biblical mandate for sexual purity. Jesus maintains that lust (committing mental adultery) is just as problematic as the act of adultery (Matt. 5:27–28).

But both are distinguished from sexual orientation. The orientation is morally neutral, since in most cases it was not chosen, and in general we are not morally culpable for actions we do not freely choose. This does not mean that sexual orientation is genetic (there is no evidence of this), but rather it is developmental, though for some people it is the only form of sexual attraction they have ever known. What this means for the believer who is same-sex oriented and wants to live faithfully to Jesus is that sexual purity is possible if he or she abstains from the behavior; a change of orientation is not required.

When it comes to same-sex marriage specifically, again the biblical teaching specifies that marriage is between one man and one woman. In Genesis 2:24, it is clear that "a man leaves his father and mother and is united to his wife, and they become one flesh." This has been the social norm for centuries, until very recently. However, just because the Bible is clear on the definition of marriage, it does not necessarily follow that the law of the land should reflect this view, at least not without a further argument to make this case. There are many behaviors that the Bible assesses as morally wrong but are not illegal. Simply because something is sin does not necessarily mean it should be illegal. For example, many sexual sins among consenting adults, such as adultery and premarital sex, are not illegal, and not many believers argue that they should be, in part because of the difficulty of enforcing such laws without intolerable invasions of privacy. Further, the law has limits in what it can do. Though it can regulate behavior, it cannot change a person's heart, which is ultimately the focus of biblical ethics.

Additionally, in a pluralistic society, the basis for civil law cannot be any one group's exclusive religious views. Any religiously based view must also be persuasive on grounds that are not entirely dependent on any particular religious revelation. That is, the law in question must be proven to advance the common good of the community or prevent clear, tangible harm to the community.

Concerning same-sex marriage and the law, there are some things to consider. First, traditional heterosexual marriage has been the consensus view for millennia, until the last few years. It has been considered foundational to social stability and the well-being of children, providing both a father and a mother, which has been considered important for the child, since mothers and fathers are not interchangeable. Mothers and fathers provide different and complementary benefits to children. For example, clear empirical evidence, accumulated over the past several decades, shows the impact of children not having fathers, including higher incidence of school dropout, juvenile delinquency, and trouble with the law. In addition, more recent studies show that stable, intact families are important for economic well-being as well.

Opponents of legalizing same-sex marriage insist that the basis for arguing for it—personal autonomy, that is, the belief that the right to love and marry whomever one chooses is a critical personal freedom—can be applied to a wide variety of other marital arrangements. For example, if autonomy is the basis, then limiting the number of marriage partners simply to one is arbitrary, opening the door to polyamory (previously known as polygamy). Further, limiting marriage partners to nonrelatives seems similarly arbitrary. On an autonomy basis, there would seem to be no reason why one could not be married to animals or to inanimate objects. All of the above scenarios have been seriously proposed by individuals seeking to exercise their marital autonomy in the aftermath of the 2015 US Supreme Court decision ruling same-sex marriage a fundamental right.

Some people have taken a bit different (and more libertarian) approach to the law on same-sex marriage, insisting that government should not be in the marriage business at all. They argue that marriage is essentially a Judeo-Christian institution and that the state has no business regulating it, except as it concerns the safety of children. That is, government should not reward or penalize people for marriage, in the tax code or otherwise. There should be neither benefits nor penalties for being married, since, they argue, such treatment discriminates against single adults, who now head the majority of households in the US. Their view is that one can hold to a moral position on marriage that defends traditional marriage and be agnostic about what the law should be. Some pastors, both in the US and around the world, are acting consistently with such a view when they consider not cooperating with the state in performing civil marriages.

TRANSGENDER

Transgender is another area in which the Bible is silent, obviously because the technology to effect sex changes did not exist in biblical times and the biblical writers could not have been expected to anticipate issues like this. But there are some principles that seem to apply to this, particularly trust in God's providence in assigning sex to individuals. Accepting one's sex as one of life's givens seems most consistent with a Christian ethic, analogous to accepting one's race and traits that are genetically determined.

Of course, not everyone who would call themselves transgender would opt for sex-change surgery. *Transgender* simply refers to a person whose gender identity is at variance with their sex at birth. This phenomenon has a variety of manifestations, ranging from cross-dressing (transvestites) to transsexuals, who desire to live full-time as members of the opposite sex. Transsexuals generally seek medical interventions to change their sex.

In some cases, a child is born with ambiguous genitalia, so it's not clear whether the child is male or female. One form of this is hermaphroditism. Ambiguous sex results from a genetic abnormality, and normally the parents select a sex at birth, which then requires corrective surgery and hormone replacement therapy. There are some medical indicators that help parents make a good decision when sex is selected. However, it seems reasonable to assume that mistakes are sometimes made in that selection, which then generates a later desire for sex change. In cases where sex change is wanted in order to correct a mistake made at birth, it would seem appropriate to allow medicine to make such a correction. That seems different from a situation in which someone is unable or unwilling to accept his or her gender as one of the givens of life.

CONCLUSION

The area of sexual ethics is fraught with controversy and ambiguities and will continue to be for the foreseeable future. This is an area of deep conflict between Christian ethics and the current cultural consensus on marriage and sexuality. Both the culture of autonomy and the high place given to the satisfaction of one's desires make adherence to a Christian sexual ethic challenging.

The Bible seems clear that sexual relations are reserved for one-man-one-woman relationships in the context of marriage. In Song of Songs, Solomon compares the sexual relationship with his bride to a garden that has been locked up (Song 4:12–16), to be opened to him following their marriage, at which time the groom is invited to taste all the choice fruits of the garden. That imagery is beautiful, evoking a vision of a garden well-tended. But gardens can also be neglected and trampled, putting them in a state of disrepair.

This imagery, though not beautiful, provides hope. Gardens presume gardeners, and the gardener in a Christian worldview is the same person who originally planted the garden—God himself. Since he is the creator of the garden, he is the one best qualified to repair it and restore it to its original beauty. This is the great hope of restoration that is part of the gospel message, that all of life, sexuality included, can be redeemed by the grace, love, and forgiveness of Christ.

Review Questions

1. Summarize the Bible's general teaching on sex and sexuality.
2. How does the Bible affirm singleness?
3. How would you respond to someone who insists that they have the right to love and have sex with whomever they choose?
4. What is the difference between contraceptive and abortifacient forms of birth control?

5. What difference does the distinction between sexual orientation and sexual behavior make in the discussion about homosexuality?

For Further Reading

Hill, Wesley. *Washed and Waiting: Reflections on Christian Faithfulness and Homosexuality.* Grand Rapids: Zondervan, 2010.

Sprinkle, Preston. *People to Be Loved: Why Homosexuality Is Not Just an Issue.* Grand Rapids: Zondervan, 2015.

Yarhouse, Mark A. *Understanding Gender Dysphoria: Navigating Transgender Issues in a Changing Culture.* Downers Grove, Ill.: IVP Academic, 2015.

CHAPTER 12

CHRISTIAN ETHICS, ECONOMICS, AND THE WORKPLACE

*How does my work connect to my
spiritual life and my service to God?*

For centuries, philosophers, economists, and theologians have reflected on the intersection of theology, work, and economics. Since most people today are in the workplace in some form (including stay-at-home moms, retirees, and volunteers), and for many it is the majority of their lives, it makes sense that Christian ethics would have a good deal to say about work and economics. After all, if the majority of our waking life is spent in the workplace, it stands to reason that the workplace would be the primary arena in which God is at work on our spiritual formation.

THE BIBLICAL STORY AND ECONOMICS

From the beginning, we learn that God created the world and called it good, making the material world fundamentally good (Gen. 1:31). He further entrusted human beings with dominion over the earth, giving them both the *privilege* of enjoying the benefits of the material world and the *responsibility* of caring for the world. We also learn that from the beginning, God has implanted his wisdom in the world and given human beings the tools necessary to uncover his wisdom and apply it for their benefit (Prov. 8:22–31). God set human beings free to utilize their God-given intelligence, initiative, and creativity in discerning and applying the wisdom he embedded in the world; this is all a part of the responsible exercise of dominion over creation, which brings innovation and productivity to benefit humankind.

The dominion mandate reflects an essential part of our being made in God's image, giving us an innate inclination to utilize the created world for productive purposes. In creation, God is portrayed as a worker (Gen. 1:31) who continues working to sustain his world. His creativity, initiative, and resourcefulness, displayed in creation, are also traits that have been given to us by virtue of our being made in his image. In addition, since the image of God is fundamentally relational, this suggests that work is intended to be embedded in relationships. We are made for cooperation and relationships as we fulfill the dominion mandate, which suggests that economic systems operate to enable those aspects of the image of God in us to flourish.

In the Old Testament law, Israel literally became a nation under God, which required a set of guidelines resembling a constitution. Many of these guidelines in the OT law have to do with economics. The purpose of Israel's "constitution" was to show how they could model God's righteousness in the way they lived together as a nation, that is, how they could become a "holy nation" (Ex. 19:5–6). When it came to economics, there were two main ways they would do this. One was to make sure their society was fair—that when people made exchanges, they did so without engaging in fraud or cheating each other (Lev. 19:35–36; Deut. 25:13–16). The law assumes that individuals could legitimately own and accumulate property, since laws prohibiting theft and fraud make sense only if something like private property is accepted. But the law also makes it clear that God is the ultimate owner of everything (Lev. 25:23; see also Ps. 24:1).

The second way that Israel would be a holy nation in terms of economics was to insure that the poor were cared for properly (Deut. 15:1–11; 26:12–13). It was assumed that people were responsible for taking care of themselves and their families. The focus in the OT law was on how to provide for people who could not provide for themselves—that was the definition of the poor. The law structured many aspects of economic life to see to it that the poor were not without opportunity to take care of themselves. For example, the law mandated a tradition known as "gleaning," in which the poor could make their way through another's agricultural field and gather some of the produce for themselves (Lev. 19:9–10). The law also provided for a right of redemption of property, so that the poor, who had met misfortune, could have renewed opportunity to make a living themselves (Lev. 25:25–28).

Finally, there was the tradition of the Year of Jubilee (Lev. 25:8–12), which returned land to its original owner every fiftieth year (though there is no evidence that such a radical tradition was ever followed, and there is substantial debate about both its original intention and its contemporary significance). The law also set forth the Sabbath tradition—based on the original creation account (Gen. 2:2)—which mandated a regular day of rest from work. One of the main purposes for this was to help the people trust God to provide for them through their six days per week of labor (Ex. 20:8–11; Deut. 5:12–15).

God's heart for the poor is revealed throughout the Psalms and other poetic literature in the OT. The marginalized, vulnerable, and oppressed occupy a special place in the heart of God, because they have only him as their defender and advocate. For example, Psalm 10:17–18 says, "You, Lord, hear the desire of the afflicted; you encourage them, and you listen to their cry, defending the fatherless and the oppressed, so that mere earthly mortals will never again strike terror." Similarly, in Psalm 82:3–4, God mandates caring for the poor and protecting them from people who would do them harm: "Defend the weak and the fatherless; uphold the cause of the poor and the oppressed. Rescue the weak and the needy; deliver them from the hand of the wicked."

The Wisdom Literature, especially the book of Proverbs, echoes this concern for the poor and oppressed. In fact, a community's care for the poor is considered an indication of how they value God:

"Whoever oppresses the poor shows contempt for their Maker, but whoever is kind to the needy honors God" (Prov. 14:31; see also Prov. 17:5; 19:17). The prophets routinely and forcefully spoke out against oppression, economic injustice, and exploitation of the poor. They considered taking care of the poor a strong indicator of a person's (and the nation of Israel's) spiritual health (Isa. 58:6–7), even making a strong connection between compassion for the poor and genuinely knowing God (Jer. 22:16)!

The prophets considered neglect of the poor a serious disregard of the law, and it was one of the symptoms of the major disease afflicting Israel: the abandonment of their relationship with God for the worship of idols and false gods (Ezek. 16:49; Amos 2:6–7; 4:1; Mic. 2:2–9; Hab. 2:6–12).

However, another important strand comes out of the Wisdom Literature, that of *individual responsibility for prosperity*. The wisdom books repeatedly make the connection between diligence, hard work, initiative—and prosperity. For example, "Lazy hands make for poverty, but diligent hands bring wealth" (Prov. 10:4). Of course, the proverbs are rules of thumb and not legal guarantees from God, so there are exceptions to this general pattern—both the poor saint and the rich idiot! And sometimes the poor are poor because they are the victims of injustice (Prov. 13:23). To be sure, this is not teaching anything like a "prosperity theology" in which God always automatically rewards righteousness with material wealth.

Even the proverbs acknowledge that wealth doesn't last forever (Prov. 27:24). But the general pattern here is that prosperity is a matter of personal responsibility—namely, hard work, diligence, and perseverance (Prov. 13:11; 14:23; 16:26; 20:13; 28:19, 20, 22, 25). The emphasis seems pretty clear—that individual responsibility, a strong work ethic, and other entrepreneurial character traits, such as initiative and perseverance, are critical to a life of economic prosperity. The proverbs illustrate this, by contrast, with the portrait of the sluggard (Prov. 26:15; 22:13; 24:30–34).

In the New Testament, the same themes are continued. The

poor were just as important to Jesus as they were to the prophets. When the followers of John the Baptist (who was in prison at the time) asked Jesus if he was indeed the Messiah who was to come, he answered in terms that could have been taken right out of the writings of the prophets. He put it like this: "Go back to John [the Baptist] and tell him what you have heard and seen—the blind see, the lame walk, those with leprosy are cured, the deaf hear, the dead are raised to life, and the Good News is being preached to the poor" (Matt. 11:4–5 NLT).

The evidence that Jesus was who he claimed to be was not only that he performed miracles but also who the beneficiaries of those miracles were—the poor, marginalized, and vulnerable. Similarly, when Jesus spoke of final judgment and what would separate his true followers from the pretenders, he made it clear that how a person treats the poor is a critical indication of his or her devotion to Jesus. This is likely what Jesus meant when, referring to feeding the hungry and taking in the needy, he said, "I tell you the truth, when you did it to the least of these my brothers and sisters, you were doing it to me!" (Matt. 25:40 NLT).

The early church carried on Jesus's pattern of caring for the poor and marginalized. They cared for the poor mainly through their extraordinary generosity, following Jesus's mandate to share freely with people who had needs (Luke 10:25–37; 12:33). They could not rely on the state to care for their poor, since the church was a persecuted minority in the Roman Empire, and since there were not many mechanisms of the state to take care of the poor. In addition, many of the early followers of Jesus were quite poor themselves. We see this amazing generosity in Acts 2:42–47. The early church "shared everything they had" (v. 44 NLT). They even sold their personal possessions and property to meet the needs of the poor among them.

This was a purely voluntary sharing and not a pattern for any *forced* redistribution of goods, which is characteristic of socialism. But there was unprecedented openhandedness with their goods, to meet needs that arose. After the day of Pentecost, in which three thousand new believers were added to the church, many of them stayed in Jerusalem to learn more about Jesus, putting a tremendous burden of hospitality on the church, which they met with amazing and Spirit-generated unselfishness. Acts 2 provides a model for this kind of personal liberality but has little to say about economic systems themselves.

In keeping with what we see in the Old Testament, self-support and personal responsibility were assumed in the early church. Self-interest was not condemned but affirmed, yet balanced by concern for the interests of others (Phil. 2:4). The responsibility of providing for one's own needs and the needs of one's family was taken very seriously. The apostle Paul encouraged a life of diligence in order to provide for self and family (1 Thess. 4:11–12), and he cautioned people who were not willing to work, saying, "Those unwilling to work will not get to eat" (2 Thess. 3:10 NLT). What he meant was that if someone was unwilling to work, he or she had no claim on the generosity of others.

Paul modeled such a life of self-support, even while he was planting churches, so he would not be a financial burden on the community. He strongly commanded idle people to "settle down and work to *earn their own living*" (2 Thess. 3:11–12 NLT). He stated this even more strongly when he told Timothy that "those who won't care for their relatives, especially those in their own household, *have denied the true faith*" (1 Tim. 5:8 NLT). This kind of personal responsibility for self-support is consistent throughout the Bible, while making room for generosity and provision for people who cannot care for themselves.

Here, then, is a summary of some of the main elements of the Bible's teaching on economic life:[1]

---

1. The previous discussion and this summary are taken from Austin Hill and Scott B. Rae, *The Virtues of Capitalism: The Moral Case for Free Markets* (Chicago: Northfield, 2010).

1. The material world is intrinsically good because it's God's good creation, though it's marred by sin.
2. God owns the world's economic resources, and human beings are trustees of those resources, responsible for their careful and productive use.
3. Responsible wealth creation is integrally connected with the dominion mandate and with the fact that human beings are made in the image of God.
4. Work and economic activity are fundamentally good, ordained by God.
5. Human beings who are capable of working are responsible for supporting themselves and their dependents.
6. The community is responsible for helping to support people who are unable to work.
7. Human beings are not to exploit the economically vulnerable but to help them support themselves.

A THEOLOGY OF WORK AND VOCATION

I teach ethics in the business school at Biola University in southern California and seminary students at Talbot School of Theology, and I routinely ask my students how people who are working in the marketplace—business professionals, blue-collar workers—are perceived in their churches, and how they tend to understand their work in the marketplace in relationship to their spiritual life. Here are some of the answers that usually come out of these discussions:

1. Work in the marketplace has value to generate revenue for the things that really matter to God—such as church work and missionary work.
2. Businesspeople are often perceived as having gifts that can help administrate the church more effectively.

3. Workplace men and women have unique opportunities to form relationships that give them the chance to share their faith with, and live out their faith among, their coworkers.

4. Workplace men and women often see themselves as not on the front lines of what God is doing in the world, as doing something "less than" for God's kingdom than what pastors or missionaries do. Often these men and women say things like, "At best, what I'm doing in the marketplace is just a support to people who are where the real action of God's kingdom is."

5. Workplace men and women often see pastors and missionaries as being in full-time ministry and see themselves as being in part-time ministry or not in ministry at all.

These views of the workplace reflect an underdeveloped theology of work and vocation. It manifests itself often in people who are in the marketplace feeling like they are doing something less for God's kingdom than what people who draw their paychecks from churches or other Christian or nonprofit organizations are doing.

INSTRUMENTAL PURPOSES FOR WORK

God calls people to the marketplace for a variety of reasons. Many of these purposes constitute what we call *instrumental value*. That is, they are useful in that they accomplish other things. For example, God calls you to work in the marketplace because you are obligated to support your family and people who are dependent on you. In addition, the Bible also suggests that we work in order to have the means to express our generosity toward the poor among us (Eph. 4:28). We also work to support the local church and the mission field. Further, in the marketplace we have an opportunity to be salt and light and to represent our faith for people who will probably never come to our churches.

But if those are the only reasons why God calls people to the marketplace, then it seems to me that we have an underdeveloped theology of work. I think the Bible teaches that work has not only instrumental value but also *intrinsic value*, specifically, value in service to Christ.

WORK HAS INTRINSIC VALUE IN SERVING CHRIST

I often ask groups of businesspeople and professional men and women, when I have a chance to speak to them, "When was work actually ordained? Was it ordained in Genesis 2 or in Genesis 3?" I'm frequently disappointed to see what an ambivalent answer is given to that question. Although most of my seminary students get this right and answer that work was ordained in Genesis 2, lots of businesspeople and professional men and women live as though work were ordained in Genesis 3. They live as though their work were their penalty, and I suspect that the vast majority of people in our churches, if they won the lottery, would quit working tomorrow.

However, the Bible is clear that work was ordained prior to the entrance of sin, and though it was cursed by sin, work itself is not a curse. In fact, in both of the biblical bookends of paradise, people are working. Adam and Eve worked beginning in Genesis 2 to till the garden, in paradise. When the Lord returns, you will still be working. When the Bible describes the kingdom being consummated after the Lord returns, the prophets use imagery like "they will beat their swords into plowshares and their spears into pruning hooks" (Isa. 2:4). The implements of war are being transformed into implements of productive work. When the kingdom is consummated, work will still be part of God's economy. In addition, at present work is being redeemed as part of the material creation being restored by the return of Christ.

To be more specific, work was ordained in Genesis 1 and 2 as one of the primary means by which human beings were to exercise dominion over creation. God also ordained procreation because Adam and Eve alone could not accomplish the task of dominion. It required a community. Throughout the process of creation, God embedded certain aspects of his wisdom in the world, and through common grace and general revelation, he's given human beings the tools to continue developing the creation and unlocking what was embedded in it. The workplace is one of the primary mechanisms by which this dominion mandate is exercised. Certainly, after the entrance of sin, dominion became immeasurably more complicated. In fact, you could probably make the case that the primary focus of dominion became alleviating and mitigating the general effects of sin. Work continues the discovery and releasing of what God embedded in creation.

Theologically, one of the main reasons why work has intrinsic value is because that's fundamentally a part of who God is, and fundamentally a part of what it means to be made in his image. From the beginning in Genesis 1, God appears as a worker. At the end of Genesis 1, he rests from his work. Throughout the Old Testament, God is portrayed as being at work to sustain and maintain his creation. Jesus, in one of his strongest claims to deity, said, "My Father is always at his work to this very day, and I too am working" (John 5:17). What this suggests, as the late Chuck Colson put it, is that as part of being made in God's image, "we are hardwired for work"; it's part of our spiritual DNA.[2] We represent the creator and creative God as we enter the workplace. Dorothy Sayers, the British author, put it like this: "Work is not what one does to live, but the thing one lives to do. It is the medium in which he or she offers himself or herself to God."[3]

The New Testament continues this idea of the intrinsic value of work. In Colossians 3:23–24, Paul puts it like this: "Whatever you

2. Charles Colson and Nancy Pearcey, *How Now Shall We Live?* (Wheaton, Ill.: Tyndale, 2000), 385.

3. Dorothy Sayers, *Why Work? Discovering Real Purpose, Peace, and Fulfillment at Work. A Christian Perspective* (CreateSpace Independent Publishing Platform, 2014), 56.

do, work at it with all your heart, as working for the Lord, not for human masters, since you know that you will receive an inheritance from the Lord as a reward. It is the Lord Christ you are serving." I think there's an implied parenthesis in v. 24: "[Whatever you do,] it is the Lord Christ you are serving." It is critical to recognize that this admonition was addressed not to pastors and missionaries but to *slaves*. In the first century, slaves did the most mind-numbing and tedious work you can imagine. Yet Paul affirms here that the work that slaves did for their masters was a part—not the whole but a part—of their service to Christ. That is, in their work as slaves, they were ultimately serving Christ, in addition to their human masters.

Now, to make sure we get this clear, I ask a lot of businesspeople, "Tell me about your ministry in the workplace." And they'll say, "Well, that happens if I lead a Bible study at lunch in my office, or if I get a chance to pray for a coworker, or on that occasion when somebody says, 'Hey, there's just something different about your life; tell me about that.'" I realized that the only things they believed constituted service to Christ in the marketplace were all those things they were doing *when they were not doing their jobs* and were actually robbing their employer of time if they did too much of it. What Paul is affirming here is that *the very work itself is a part of their service to Christ*. It doesn't exhaust their service to him, because men and women have service obligations in lots of other arenas besides the marketplace, such as their families, neighborhoods, and local churches.

But the work itself that people are doing is a part of their service to Christ. Take a look at the term ministry; in the Greek New Testament, it's the term *diakonia*, which is frequently translated "service" as well as "ministry." For example, in Acts 6:1–6, the ministry of waiting on tables is described as a diakonia in the same way that the ministry of preaching and prayer is described as a diakonia. Of course, they were different things that different people were called to do because of what God wanted them to do, but both of those things are called ministry. I think the best way to refer to that is, they were different arenas of service to which people were called.

Think about it this way: If it's true that what people in the marketplace are doing is service to Christ, then men and women in the workplace are doing God's work in the world, analogous to pastors doing God's work in the local church, and missionaries doing God's work in the mission field. If that's true, then what goes on in the marketplace also has eternal significance.

So the person who understands this theologically can't say, "Well, I'm a [machine tool operator or construction builder or something like that], just drilling holes to put nails in" or use other language to express that his or her work is not particularly significant. What goes on in the marketplace is an arena of service to Christ, which gives it part of its eternal significance. That's why we say, both to pastors and to workplace men and women, that yes, pastoring is ministry, but accounting is ministry, and filmmaking is ministry, and marketing is ministry, and music is ministry. When my students tell me, "I left my business to go into full-time ministry," I like to say gently, "No, you've done nothing of the sort." The reason for this is that all Christ followers are in full-time service to him, and whether a person is in full-time service or not has nothing to do with where he or she gets a paycheck.

At what point do all Christ followers enter full-time service to him? It's at the moment when a person comes to faith. When you change jobs, you simply change arenas of service. When a pastor steps down from a pastorate, what do we usually say? That they've "left the ministry." Actually, they have not. They have, like the workplace person, simply changed arenas of service. So all of us, if we are followers of Jesus, are in full-time service to Christ, and where you get a paycheck is a different issue than whether you're in full-time ministry.

I think the way we talk about this makes a big difference in contributing to this sense that businesspeople and marketplace people have that they're doing something "less than" for God's kingdom. I try never to use the term *full-time ministry* to refer to any specific occupation. I certainly try not to use it in reference to the pastorate or the mission field. Because what that implies to the person in the marketplace is that they're either in part-time ministry or not in ministry at all. Neither of those things are true theologically.

CONCLUSION

Sometime ago, a longtime friend of mine and his wife were coming back from vacation, and on the jetway as they were departing from the plane, she collapsed, blacked out, regained consciousness, and then was sort of in and out of consciousness for a while. They rushed her to a neurologist and found out that a tumor about the size of a quarter at the base of her brain was causing these blackouts. Through a brand-new technology called the "gamma knife," they were able to excise the tumor in a single outpatient surgical procedure. She went home that same day and to my knowledge is totally fine today.

I remember my friend reflecting on all the occupations that had to come together to facilitate his wife's healing, and he was particularly taken with the team or individual (probably a team) that had written the imaging software that enabled the neurosurgeon to pinpoint where the tumor was and to get it out with a minimum of damage. I remember the statement my friend made. He said, "Assuming that person is a Christian, I am so glad that the person who wrote that imaging software didn't decide to leave his business to go serve the Lord full-time." I think what he meant by this was, he recognized that in the providence of God, that person was part of a team that helped accomplish the very important task of healing for his wife.

I think my friend recognized what Paul affirmed to slaves and what I think we need to affirm to men and women in the marketplace. For those of you who are pastoring, we need to affirm this to marketplace people in your churches and in the groups of people whom God has entrusted to your care: it is the Lord Christ whom they are serving in their work. To do this, we need to stop talking about full-time ministry, vocational ministry, professional ministry, secular jobs, entering and leaving the ministry, and higher callings. I would suggest not using the term *ministry* without a qualifier that specifies the arena of service. All of us are in full-time service, regardless of where our paycheck comes from.

Review Questions

1. What are the main elements of the Bible's teaching on economics?
2. When in the Bible did God ordain work? In Genesis 2 or Genesis 3? What difference does your answer make to your view of work?
3. How would you use the Bible's teaching to defend the nobility of work as a form of service to Christ?
4. True or false: All Christ followers are in full-time ministry.

For Further Reading

Nelson, Tom. *Work Matters: Connecting Sunday Worship to Monday Work.* Wheaton, Ill.: Crossway, 2011.

Rae, Scott B., and Kenman L. Wong. *Beyond Integrity: A Judeo-Christian Approach to Business Ethics,* 3rd ed. Grand Rapids: Zondervan, 2012.

Van Duzer, Jeff. *Why Business Matters to God (And What Still Needs to Be Fixed).* Downers Grove, Ill.: InterVarsity Press, 2010.

Wong, Kenman L., and Scott B. Rae. *Business for the Common Good: A Christian Vision for the Marketplace.* Downers Grove, Ill.: IVP Academic, 2011.

SUBJECT INDEX

SCRIPTURE INDEX

Page numbers in italics indicate where verses or parts of verses are quoted.